eXpand Your Business Using eBay

eXpand Your Business Using eBay

J.S. McDougall

EP
Entrepreneur® Press

Editorial Director: Jere Calmes
Cover Design: Desktop Miracles, Inc.
Editorial Development and Production: CWL Publishing Enterprises, Inc., Madison, WI, www.cwlpub.com

This publication is designed to provide accurate and authoritative information in regard to the subject matter covered. It is sold with the understanding that the publisher is not engaged in rendering legal, accounting, or other professional services. If legal advice or other expert assistance is required, the services of a competent professional person should be sought.
—From a Declaration of Principles jointly adopted by a Committee of the American Bar Association and a Committee of Publishers and Associations

Registered with the Libary of Congress.

12 11 10 09 08 07   10 9 8 7 6 5 4 3 2 1

dEdication

To Edie and Cally
… for their help with this project

Contents

iNtroduction

As a small business owner, you are no doubt familiar with the two most basic elements of running any business: hard work and risk. Selling on eBay is no exception. eBay is an open marketplace with hundreds of millions of buyers. Remaining profitable while selling to those buyers will require sometimes fierce day-to-day, head-to-head competition with other eBay sellers. It is hard work, and, as with any business venture, there is risk. This book will guide business owners through the maze of selling on eBay. There are ways for you to minimize risk and maximize the effectiveness of your hard work. This book will show you how.

Make no mistake, eBay has created an inspired—and inspiring—selling platform. Where else in the world can any small business in the world compete on a level playing ground with big-timers like IBM, Disney, and General Motors? Whether you run one of these gigantic multinational corporations, or an antique bookstore above a flower shop, eBay will provide you with the same management tools, the same access to buyers, and the same advertising opportunities. eBay gives the underdog a shot at the title.

tHe mArketplace

eBay's selling potential is unmatched by any marketplace—physical or digital—ever created. The site's global reach, ease of use, and low cost of entry combine to create the most powerful sales engine the world has ever seen. By expanding your business to sell on eBay, you will be able to tap into the huge potential created by eBay's hundreds of millions of online shoppers who are looking every day for quality products.

As this book will show you, eBay is no longer strictly an auction site for individuals. eBay has evolved over the years to include not only baseball cards and Pez dispensers, but also new cars, computers, Christmas stockings, and everything in between. Today, hundreds of thousands of small businesses are participating in, and finding success selling on, eBay. Even large corporations such as Disney, Pepsico, and General Motors are finding that is worth their time and money to set up shop selling in the world's largest marketplace.

Learning how to effectively market your company on eBay—the strategies, pitfalls, and huge opportunities—will be worthwhile for you and your business. In many cases expanding to sell on eBay can be done successfully with a nominal investment of time and money. In some cases, it will prove more difficult. In either case, though, if you are able to master the techniques and tools provided in this book, there's almost no limit to the amount of growth your business can achieve.

eBay hIstory

eBay's story of growth has attained legend status in Internet commerce circles, and Pierre Omidyar—eBay's founder—is the legend's hero. Omidyar started the auction site in 1995 as Auction Web. It launched as a small subsection of a web site for Echo Bay Technology Group—Omidyar's private consulting practice. His original intention was to place his consulting web site at echobay.com, but he learned upon trying to register it that it was already in use by Echo Bay Mines, a gold mining company in Canada's Northwest Territory. He settled for an abbreviated version: eBay.com.

In the first months of operation, Auction Web was just a simple auction program that enabled individuals to buy and sell items online. Omidyar chose an auction format because he felt it was the fairest method for determining an item's selling price. The legend goes that Omidyar realized the potential of his creation when he was able to sell a broken laser pointer to a broken laser pointer collector for $13.83. Bizarre transactions such as this proved that Auction Web had a powerful ability to connect buyers and sellers in a way that no other platform had achieved previously. Auction Web was one of the first programs to leverage the full power of the Internet.

Auction Web enjoyed some success in its first years. The number of registered users spiked so quickly that Omidyar had trouble keeping the server from crashing. The company hired its first employee, Chris Agarpao, and brought on Stanford Business School graduate Jeff Skoll to become the company's first president. By the time Auction Web was changed to eBay in 1997, the company had already grown to have 341,000 registered users and $95,000 in annual gross sales.

In 1998 Meg Whitman was hired as the company's second president. Skoll became the company's vice president of Strategic Planning and Analysis. By the time Whitman came to eBay, she had already amassed an impressive resume, which included Proctor & Gamble, Walt Disney Company, Stride Rite, FTD Florists, and Hasbro. She immediately put her experience to work. In Whitman's first year the company's annual gross sales grew by nearly 800%, finishing off at $745,000. eBay's number of registered users passed 2 million.

Whitman's arrival ushered in years of exponential growth. The company began buying up competing and complimentary companies, both in the United States and overseas. In 1998, eBay bought auction site up4sale.com. In 1999, they purchased online payment processor BillPoint, and auction houses Butterfield & Butterfield and Alando. Between the years of 2000 and 2006, eBay had purchased over 17 new companies, most of which they disbanded, but those that they found useful—PayPal, Half.com, Shopping.com, Skype—they integrated into their own eBay services.

At the end of 2006, eBay was operating in 26 countries around the world, owned marketplace, financial, and communications companies, and, according to NetCraft, was the 12th most visited site on the Internet.

It hasn't been effortless growth on eBay's part. They've needed to constantly battle fraud, shill bidding, unscrupulous auctions, spam, and lawsuits. But despite the hardships it faces, eBay is able to provide such a popular and profitable service that it continues to grow into new markets, new countries, and new directions.

eBay and bUsinesses

While eBay was launched with the idea that it would help individual sellers auction off their used goods, eBay has grown over the years to be much more versatile. Large computer hardware businesses such as IBM, Sun Microsystems, and Hewlett-Packard were early to recognize the huge selling potential that eBay presented for their business equipment. As early as 2001, Sun Microsystems had successfully sold over $10 million worth of its equipment on eBay. These early corporate adopters paved the way for smaller businesses to sell on eBay by opening up the then-resistant eBay shopping community to retail items with higher average sales prices.

As soon as retail sellers took an interest in selling on eBay, the company responded. They embraced this influx of retail goods from business sellers by launching the eBay Stores program on June 11, 2001. This new selling format allowed sellers to avoid putting their items through the regular auction process, which could last up to 10 days. Instead, sellers were able to able to place items at a fixed price in their customized eBay Stores, where shoppers could buy their items immediately. This new fixed-price format provided sellers guaranteed profits per sale—something that established businesses needed to see before making the leap to eBay.

After eBay Stores proved to be a huge success with both buyers and sellers, eBay launched a fixed-price non-store option in 2002. This new fixed-price format listing was included in the regular search results among all the other auctions. It allowed sellers who didn't care to pay for an eBay Stores subscription to sell items at a fixed price. In 2006, eBay expanded on its one-stop-shop image by launching eBay Express.

eBay Express is one of eBay's specialty sites—meaning it has its own web address (ebayexpress.com) and can stand entirely on its own. This new specialty site is essentially an eBay shopping mall, stocked exclusively—and automatically—with brand-new items from eBay's PowerSellers. All the items listed are available for immediate purchase, as the site does not delve into the world of auctions at all—hence the name "Express."

These new additions to eBay's selling platform are created entirely with small retail businesses in mind. eBay only stands to gain by attracting the world's retailers to sell to its 212 million registered users, and therefore they are making it easier than ever for established businesses to sell through their site. eBay's listing management programs, such as Selling Manager Pro, Blackthorne Pro, and the new TurboLister 2.0, have matured and are now sophisticated and powerful management applications. New import/export abilities make it easier than ever to integrate eBay sales into your current sales software. And, with the thousands of third-party programs available, you'll have plenty of management solutions from which to choose.

eBay sells approximately $3.15 billion worth of goods for its sellers every month. This translates to $1,197 worth of goods every second—an impressive and much-touted statistic that you'll likely encounter often in your research. With over 28,000 different item categories, there is certainly a niche on eBay in which your business can excel. In the following chapters, this book will outline the process, describe the management tools available, and provide examples to guide you in the expansion of your business to the exciting world of eBay.

eBay and Your bUsiness

As mentioned above, eBay boasts over 28,000 item categories. These categories range everywhere from real estate to cell phones to stamps. Take a look through Appendix A to see if one of eBay's categories is a good match for your business—chances are that you'll find several. Once you determine the best categories for your products, go to eBay and browse through the items in that category. You'll see many familiar products, many of which might be exactly what you sell from your own business, but don't let that dissuade you. There is plenty of room within eBay's 212 million users for more sellers, and even though competition can become fierce within the microcosm of one category, you already have an upper hand over all the sellers—you're already in the business. This helps you in many ways.

First, eBay is based on the idea that users will trust perfect strangers with their goods and their hard-earned money. If trust breaks down between the buyer and an unknown seller, no sale will take place. The site's feedback star rating system goes a long way to instill shoppers with confidence when buying from strangers, but it does not always seal the deal. Buyers expect more assurance from sellers than what a colorful star can offer. This is where your business can excel.

In truth, people shop with perfect strangers every day. When was the last time you greeted the owner of the local Barnes & Noble by name? Or sent holiday cards to the butcher at Stop'n'Shop? The chances are that it hasn't ever happened. But we still trust these perfect strangers to provide us with professional service precisely because they are professionals. We trust them because the established period of time they've been in business speaks to their credibility as a seller. The same dynamic is at work on eBay. Your established business already has more credibility with eBay buyers than hordes of individual sellers who might very well be reselling somebody else's items from their mother's basement. People prefer to shop with established businesses, and they are willing to pay a little more for the assurance of good quality and better service.

The second way in which having an established business gives you a leg up on the competition is that you know your products. You have been working with your product line and the customers of your product line long enough to know the quirks of the items—and customers. This intimate knowledge of your industry will help you provide a level of customer service that is often all too rare on eBay. eBay buyers expect an e-mail here and there throughout the purchasing process, and they hope they'll have some recourse if the item isn't as they expected— which sometimes they have, and sometimes they don't. If a sale goes south, buyers chalk it up to "well, that's eBay." This reflects eBay's poor average standard of customer service. With your business's ability to speak intelligently about your products, answer the phone during business hours, and answer e-mails promptly, you will be able to blow much of the competition in your category out of the water. This book will show you how to create item listings and an eBay Store that immediately show buyers that you run a professional and reliable business.

Third, as you've been selling your products for some time, you have established relationships with reliable suppliers. Most eBay sellers buy items when and where they can, and sell them for whatever they can get. It's a mish-mashed way to do business, and it makes for inconsistent product lines and unreliable product availability. You can offer eBay buyers something more. Reliable and well-thought-out product lines will make you popular with eBay shoppers. Many businesses that have expanded to eBay no longer put items up for auction. Their eBay Stores have become so popular with shoppers that they have a steady stream of repeat customers for their fixed-price items at retail prices.

eBay is adapting to this demand and is working to include more businesses. The more reliable the eBay sellers are, the better off eBay will be. Now, as eBay is making moves to attract business sellers, is a great time to take your experience and knowledge in your industry to selling on eBay. The eBay buyers are hungry for better products and better service, and you stand in a great position to provide both.

Finally, you are in a great position to sell on eBay because you already have many of the management systems already in place. Individual eBay sellers starting from scratch still need to work out the kinks and processes of managing their inventory, creating a customer database, finding a sales manager program, and so forth. These are things you've tackled already. Integrating eBay into many of these systems is as easy as adding new sales.

gOals of sElling on eBay

There's no point to expanding your business to any market if it is going to be more trouble than it's worth. Increasing the size of your business should not increase the size of your stress headache. As a small business owner, you are no doubt often stressed, insanely busy, and worried about finances. Selling on eBay is not the cure for all these ailments, despite what some Internet advertisements might tell you. But expanding to eBay shouldn't increase these problems, and in some cases it will help.

Increasing Profits

One of the most attractive aspects of selling on eBay is that it is an inexpensive way to expand your business. You will not need to rent or buy space for another retail location. You will not need to hire a slew of new employees. You will not need to cough up cash to double your inventory. Much of what needs to be done to sell on eBay can be done with your existing infrastructure, your existing employees, and existing inventory. eBay is simply a means of selling your products to millions of new customers through your Internet connection.

There will be some investment required, of course, especially in the beginning phases. It takes a lot of time and work to create photos and descriptions for every item in your inventory. Employees will need to be given new tasks, or you may need to hire one or two new people. And space in your shop will need to be dedicated to a new "eBay department"—a department that may be merely a cubicle, or an entire warehouse.

eBay charges no setup fee, no registration fee, no monthly fees, and many of the best eBay management tools are free. PayPal, an online payment processor popular on eBay, also charges no start-up fees and no monthly fees. The price you pay for doing business on eBay is largely per transaction. eBay charges fees to list items, and a fee based on the final selling value of any item sold. PayPal also charges a per-transaction fee, but it is comparable with credit card terminal rates, and only applies if buyers choose to pay though PayPal.

Due to the pay-per-transaction nature of selling on eBay, your expansion venture can be immediately profitable for your business. This book will show you the best ways to keep selling fees low and employee time efficient to make sure you get the most profit per sale.

Finding New Markets

If you've operated your business solely out of a physical retail space, you have enormous opportunity just waiting to be tapped. If there is enough interest for your products to support your business in your local market, then there is substantial interest in your products in other places in the world as well. eBay can be your connection to those new markets. Pierre Omidyar's discovery of the broken laser pointer collector serves as a good example of hidden markets.

In another example, Biz Paris, whom you will learn more about later in this book, operates the West Barnstable Trading Company—a wonderful antique shop in West Barnstable, Massachusetts. Since the 1970s she has operated out of a tiny meeting house in a small town on Cape Cod. She caters to tourists mostly and the occasional local antique or bargain hunter. She began selling on eBay only at the insistence of a local friend. As soon as she got started, the window shutters that had been cluttering up her back room began to sell like hot cakes. They sold so well, and she had so many, that packing and shipping the bulky shutters began to take up too much of her time. Now she only lists the shutters during her slower winter months when she has the time and can use the extra money.

If your business has operated from one, or several, retail locations and through your own company web site, you have done well to cover several markets. But as you have no doubt learned, retail sales can be a burden on your employees' time and on your budget. Spending your day fitting an uncooperative nine-year-old into countless pairs of shoes can be frustrating and expensive when you calculate what your time is worth. Sales from your web site are easier to handle. There are no screaming kids, most communication is done over e-mail, and you need only pack up the item and send it away. But getting customers to visit your web site is a constant struggle. Internet advertising is expensive and becoming more difficult. There are tricks that you hear people talking about but you have no time to learn how to make these sometimes technical changes. The process of choosing keywords and landing pages and specific site text can be confusing and frustrating as well.

eBay provides you with a great opportunity to place your products right into the middle of millions of shoppers. eBay provides the site traffic. eBay provides the secure checkout. eBay even provides the traffic and sales reports. You need only learn how to best place your products within eBay, and the sales will begin to flow in from new buyers in new markets on which you will be able to focus your attention. Who knew there was a severe need for window shutters in Florida? Or that there was a Society of Broken Laser Pointers in Boise? People have incorporated eBay into their shopping routines. Placing your items where people are searching is a great way to find new opportunities.

gOals of tHis bOok

It would be easy to tell you that if you put this book under your pillow tonight you'd wake up tomorrow an Internet millionaire. But, sadly, it wouldn't be true. This book will serve as merely a guide to selling on eBay. The hard work must come from beyond these pages. It is true that eBay makes it easy to begin selling through their service, but it is not easy to make millions on the site. In order to be successful as an eBay seller you will need to study eBay, study selling techniques, study product placement, and study your own management practices. Only a few sellers in eBay's history have found the keys necessary for exponential growth of profits. The rest are finding success by tweaking their strategies, refining their product lines, watching their costs, and outperforming the competition.

This book will help you understand the eBay landscape. It will detail the process of getting started, the tools that are necessary for efficient sales, and the common pitfalls of beginner and experienced sellers. This book covers the most reliable strategies for maximizing your items' visibility within eBay, how to convert sales once an item is seen, and how to maximize profits once the sale is made.

There are many books and many hucksters in the market promising instant fortune on eBay. Their titles and pitches would have you believing that eBay is still undiscovered and waiting anxiously for an enterprising individual to come in and claim its millions. This guide is different. Yes, there are great opportunities for businesses on eBay, particularly now. But this book alone will not capture those opportunities for you. The goal of this book is to provide you with the tools and knowledge that other businesses that have made the leap to eBay have learned to be valuable.

To that end, this book follows the eBay expansion process undertaken by Trumbull Mountain Tack Shop, a horse tack shop in southwestern Vermont. The folks at Trumbull Mountain were gracious enough to allow their expansion experiences to serve throughout this book as examples for your business. It was not a seamless, smooth road for Trumbull Mountain, and so much the better. Your expansion process will be smoother for it. In the following chapters you'll learn about the mistakes, problems, and lessons that Trumbull Mountain encountered on their bumpy path to eBay success.

The Book's Boxes

Throughout the book you will notice boxes that call your attention to important information. These boxes serve to provide you with quick tips and other helpful bits of advice from eBay sellers. The types of boxes you will are:

Helpful Hint. These Helpful Hint boxes will contain tips that you can put to immediate use to make this process easier. They might include helpful software, helpful advice, or a friendly caution.

Strategy Snippet. The Strategy Snippets are bits of helpful strategic advice. Use these snippets to refine your eBay selling strategy for maximum efficiency and effectiveness.

Trumbull's Stumbles. Trumbull Mountain Tack Shop learned a lot in their expansion process, much of which will be useful for you to know before you get started yourself. These Trumbull's Stumbles boxes will contain advice about avoiding common pitfalls.

Trumbull Mountain Tack Shop

Trumbull Mountain Tack Shop, Inc. has been selling high-quality saddles, bits, bridles, girths, pads, and other riding equipment for equestrians for over 30 years. The business currently has three full-time, and several part-time, employees. Edie Tschorn is the shop's owner and it is because of her that this book is able to use her company's experience expanding to eBay as an example for your transition. We are grateful to her for her generosity and patience.

Trumbull Mountain Tack Shop

To learn more about Trumbull Mountain Tack Shop visit their eBay Store and web site at the addresses below. If you're in the area, they invite you to stop in!
969 Trumbull Hill Road
Shaftsbury, Vermont 05262
Store Hours:
Sunday through Friday, 11 am to 5 pm
Saturdays, 9 am to 5 pm
Telephone: 802-442-9672
Toll-Free: 800-442-8672
Web Site: www.trumbullmtn.com
E-mail: saddles@trumbullmtn.com
eBay Username: trumbullmtn
eBay Store: Trumbull-Mountain-Tack-Shop
eBay Store URL: http://stores.ebay.com/Trumbull-Mountain-Tack-Shop

Trumbull Mountain Tack Shop's History

Trumbull Mountain Tack Shop got its start in 1976 as Trumbull Mountain Stables. Edie grew up on the Vermont farm on which the business now resides. The farm, which has been in Edie's family for three generations, spreads out over the rolling hilltop hayfields of Shaftsbury, Vermont. From the highest hayfield, one can see straight down the valley into the larger town of Bennington, several miles to the south. To the west, the rolling landscape of upstate New York can be seen in the distance. Farms and barnyards dot the surrounding hills.

As is true of so many farms in Vermont, this land was originally used by Edie's ancestors as a dairy farm. In the early 1960s Edie's family, along with many other small Vermont dairy operations, found that it had become impossible to turn a profit in the shadow of larger, industrial dairy facilities. It became clear that they needed to sell their herd.

Edie has spent much energy over the years reworking the fields and cow facilities to accommodate her large passion for horses. Pastures were replaced with hayfields, fences were strung with electricity, and horse stalls were squeezed into any available nook and cranny of the barn. Intent on making her living working with horses, Edie opened up the newly minted horse farm to the local community. Fellow horse owners were invited to board their horses with Edie, who made sure they were well cared for and well fed. Horse owners had access to the fields and new horse trails during the day and Edie tucked in the horses at night. Edie found the endeavor to be emotionally rewarding, but financially underwhelming. She often found it a struggle to keep the business profitable.

As the central figure in this new horse enthusiast community, Edie found that she had become the default owner of a lot of horse tack and supplies that had been left behind or otherwise abandoned by customers. At a loss for what to do with the collective mess, she piled it all together in the corner of the old barn and stuck a "For Sale" sign on the top of it—and thus, Trumbull Mountain Tack Shop was born.

The items in the pile sold quickly. Encouraged, Edie began to over-order her regular supplies—brushes, soap, treats—and place them on some shelves above where her old pile had been. When these extra horse-care supplies sold quickly as well, Edie submitted a larger order for more items with more variety.

Over time, Edie sectioned off a space in the barn to accommodate strictly her item sales. She outgrew this spot in the old barn and finally moved the whole operation to the second floor of a new barn she had recently built on the property. She added saddles, tack, a cash register, and, in time, expanded to the Internet. She hired intelligently, recruiting people from the local horse community who knew as much as, or more than, she did about saddles and saddle fitting.

The tack shop today still operates out of the second floor of the "new" horse barn—though the space has been through considerable remodeling and modernization. They do roughly 80% of their business through the company's web site at **www.trumbullmtn.com**. The remaining business comes in the form of foot traffic from visitors from all over the Northeast. The experience that Edie has, and has filled her business with, has made Trumbull Mountain Tack Shop extremely popular with horse lovers around the world. She regularly receives repeat orders from as far away as California, England, and Japan. People appreciate Trumbull Mountain's knowledge, flexibility, and professionalism. It is exactly these traits that Edie hopes will make her business a success on eBay.

Trumbull Mountain's Goals on eBay

Like other businesses making the move to selling on eBay, Trumbull Mountain hopes to achieve the general goals of increasing sales, profits, and market percentage, though it was a few more immediate goals that Trumbull Mountain had that drew Edie to eBay.

Trumbull Mountain's web site draws a respectable 5,000 unique visitors every month. These customers are largely searching for new saddles, used saddles, and the associated tack. While Trumbull Mountain's web site has been extremely effective for them—as mentioned above, it accounts for 80% of sales—it does not allow for online purchasing. It offers no e-commerce of any kind. Customers interested in buying a saddle from the company must contact Trumbull Mountain either by e-mail or over the telephone. Edie came to realize that the 80 to 100 new customers she received every month paled in comparison to the number of people viewing the web site every month. She attributed the huge difference to the fact that in today's technological atmosphere, when people are so accustomed to buying online, her old-fashioned method of asking customers to pick up the phone was standing as a barrier to sales. Edie needed a way of allowing customers to buy online.

In addition to Edie, Trumbull Mountain has only two full-time employees. As you can imagine, they are both kept quite busy with their usual duties. The company's part-time web-master maintained the Trumbull Mountain site in her spare time after she finished at her full-time job. She did not have the time to implement a full-scale e-commerce web site. And Edie had no desire to spend thousands of dollars paying someone to create a web site that, upon launch, she'd have no idea how to operate.

There are many pre-made store programs available across the Internet. None but eBay have the reputation for being home to legitimate sellers. And none but eBay offer millions of potential customers instantly upon registration. Edie decided that eBay was the only way to go for offering quick, secure, online sales.

ꜰRom the ₐUthor

Like you, I am interested in eBay. I love to read success stories about small businesses in Smalltown, USA who have found success like never before selling on eBay. I am inspired by the entrepreneurs who take a chance, risk their day jobs, and come out more prosperous than they ever thought possible on the other side. eBay has produced more of these stories than any other marketplace in the world.

I am lucky that my job is to seek out these intrepid entrepreneurs and learn their stories, their inspirations, and their methods for success. I feel doubly lucky that I am then able to pass on their methods and inspirations to even more intrepid entrepreneurs like you, anxious to find your own path to success.

If you find that this book has helped you along your expansion to eBay, I would love to hear from you. Please send an e-mail with your stories, thoughts, corrections, or concerns to ebay@jsmcdougall.com.

Also, the sellers featured in this book have devoted much of their time and energy to helping me, and you. They were not, by any means, obligated to share their experiences—in fact, they had good reason not to, as sharing their secrets for success will only make their eBay competition stronger. They devoted their time in the hopes that they could help a fellow entrepreneur and business owner find success on eBay as well. Please visit their eBay Stores, and, if you can, contribute to their business. They deserve our gratitude. Thank you.

Now on with the adventure!

eXpand Your
Business Using
eBay

PowerSellers

Over the course of conducting research for this book, I spoke with dozens of eBay sellers—both large and small—who all had their own way of doing things. Trumbull Mountain, whom I mentioned in the introduction, was but one of the helpful sellers who were excited to help new sellers succeed through this book. In this chapter, I'll introduce you to two more eBay businesses—one tiny and one huge.

Both of the following sellers came to eBay as a method for expanding their current businesses. Both of them developed very different methods for selling on eBay. And both of them have found success. So whether you're planning to be a small business selling on eBay to subsidize your cash flow, a medium-sized seller using eBay to create growth, or a PowerSeller leveraging eBay as a main source of revenue, there is a sample business in this book to help guide you.

sMall and sImple

Biz Parris started selling antiques and collectibles back in 1979 as a source of quick income after losing a job. She purchased an old meeting house on Cape Cod to double as her store and home. Over the years her business, the West Barnstable Trading Company, has grown

The West Barnstable Trading Company has been serving local bargain and treasure hunters since 1979.

beyond antiques to include collectibles, furniture, art, glassware, pottery, and more. She has stuffed every corner and crevice of the meeting house—from floor to rafters—with treasures from around the world.

The tourist season is quite busy on Cape Cod and can provide Biz with considerable foot traffic. Treasure seekers hunt through the overflowing shelves and tables and rooms looking for that one perfect item that's buried within the many piles that are organized in a way that I suspect only Biz truly understands. Biz's collection is so large and so varied that her customers are rarely disappointed. Her store has the feel of a place where it wouldn't be surprising to see Indiana Jones step out of the back room, hat in hand.

Biz was at first resistant to the idea of selling on the Internet, which a friend and neighbor of hers insisted she should explore. She didn't own a computer. She didn't know how to use one. And she didn't know whether the effort would be worth the investment. Finally in 1999, after much prodding, she relented. Her friend built her a computer, taught her the basics, and got Biz up and running. She began listing her items for sale on Amazon's early attempt at a marketplace. After finding little success there, and after hearing about the huge potential of a new auction site, she moved to eBay.

One of the many overflowing sets of shelves, and Biz's simple inventory storage system

eBay was immediately more successful for Biz than Amazon's marketplace. She undertook the huge endeavor of photographing each item in her store and listing them for auction. She listed every item directly through eBay's web site, just as she does today. She finds that she has become so familiar over the years with the eBay web site that it is faster and easier (and less expensive) for her to submit listings directly through the site than through "the fancy tools" that charge monthly fees.

Biz found that eBay was a great avenue for sales. Her online sales quickly grew to outnumber her in-store sales and remained that way for the next few years. In 2005 Biz was selling a large number of items through eBay, but she found that for the amount of work she was putting into photographing, describing, listing, and shipping, her new sales were not producing the profits she had hoped.

Instead of throwing in the towel and declaring that eBay sales weren't worth the effort, Biz decided to refine her selling strategies. She examined her eBay sales for the previous few years and found two problems: her average sale price was too low, and she spent a great deal of time dealing with extremely particular customers.

Biz solved these two problems overnight. She stopped listing any and all items below a certain dollar value. And she stopped listing the items that usually sold to picky collectors, such as books. As a consequence, Biz instantly doubled her average selling price and significantly reduced the amount of time she spent answering questions from customers. Over the next year, due to these two simple changes, Biz doubled her eBay income.

_s_Trategy _s_Nippet

Biz finds that ending her auctions on Sunday between 10 am and 2 pm Pacific Standard Time yields her the highest final sale prices. During that time, she says, eBay has high traffic from both the east and west coasts.

Biz now leaves the items that cause her the most trouble—collector's items, clothing, and items that require intricate packing—to the winter months, when the tourist traffic on the cape slows down and she has more time to deal with them.

Biz runs her business effectively by herself. She has one part-time employee, and she drives all her sales to the post office every day. When asked about saving time through UPS's pickup service she said she likes going to the post office; it gives her a chance to leave the store and talk with the other ladies there.

Today, eBay accounts for 75 to 80% of Biz's business. She enjoys the people she meets through the site, the convenience of PayPal, and the discovery of new markets for her items. She has earned the rank of eBay PowerSeller, and now sells both through auctions and through an eBay store. She has two external web sites, both of which point visitors to her eBay items, and she is looking for new methods of marketing and new selling strategies every day. eBay, she confesses, is the reason she's able to stay in business.

Ken (right) and Nathan of Blue Star Computer Corporation

eNormous and eFficient

As is common with so many start-up businesses, Blue Star Computer Corporation got its start in the basement of the owner, Ken. The idea when it launched in 1994, as it is now, was to sell original-equipment replacement components for proprietary computer systems. For example, many companies equip their employees with specific model notebook computers—say the new Sony TXN17P/T. The TXN17P/T is a sleek, small, ultra-portable computer with all the wireless bells and whistles, and it is therefore very popular with both large corporations and consumers. However, to achieve that sleek, small, ultra-portable design Sony needed to custom design a DVD drive that they could stuff into the tiny computer. This left companies (and regular consumers) with a problem when the DVD drive in their TXN17P/T failed. As no other companies make a DVD drive that will fit the TXN17P/T, their only option was to order an expensive replacement directly from Sony. This scenario repeats itself for consumers and companies all over the world with all types of computer equipment, many of whom see this as an undesirable situation.

For owners of older computers, the problem of replacing proprietary hardware is only worse. Companies like Sony and Dell and IBM often decide to discontinue selling replacement parts for their computers only a few years after the sale of the original computer. This leaves companies and consumers without recourse when a computer component fails in their system. This is the problem that Blue Star solves.

Blue Star buys up old inventories of proprietary computer systems from companies that are either going out of business or upgrading their computer systems. These computers from large manufacturers are still filled with quality, working parts when the original purchasing company chooses to offload them. Blue Star tests each computer, dismantles them all for parts, and sells the working components for specific computer models to the people who need replacement parts. Because they purchase unwanted computer systems, and have created such an efficient system for recycling these parts, Blue Star can offer parts at a fraction of the price that the original manufacturers charge. It is a brilliant concept and has been working for Blue Star for many years.

Until relatively recently, Blue Star sold mainly from its own web site at **www.bluestarusa.com**. In 2000, Blue Star decided to give eBay a try and hired experienced eBay seller Nathan White to help them out. From what I can see, Nathan has done most everything right— from the design of Blue Star's eBay auctions, to the integration of eBay sales into Blue Star's existing systems.

Blue Star, as you may have inferred, has moved out of Ken's basement. They are now located in a retail and warehouse space in an industrial park in Holliston, Massachusetts, southwest of Boston. Nathan manages the company's eBay sales from a cluttered desk in the front of the business.

Just this one aisle in Blue Star's warehouse is packed with thousands of replacement parts for proprietary computer systems. Companies around the world need these parts to keep their computer systems running.

Nathan's desk doubles as his simple photo studio for the small items they sell.

Nathan scours the company's inventory list every day searching for new potentially profitable items. When he finds one that he thinks could turn a profit, he checks eBay's completed listings to gauge the final selling price of similar items. If he finds that the average sale price on eBayof an item is higher than what Blue Start purchased it for, he puts it up for auction. This tactic reduces the company's risk for making an unprofitable sale.

Nathan has spent so much time stocking and refining the company's eBay store that the business now does 95% of its eBay sales as fixed-price through the store—guaranteeing a profitable sale every time. Only the company's rare or incredibly in-demand items go up for auction.

This low-auction strategy only works for Blue Star because they have established themselves as an honest, reputable company and therefore have a large following of repeat customers who go directly to the Blue Star eBay Store. Also, as Blue Star sells replacement parts for, mostly, corporate computer systems, the technicians who make up the bulk of their customers often need the replacement parts immediately. Blue Star has fine-tuned their strategy to meet the needs of their customers. This is a strategy that also saves the company thousands of dollars every year because the eBay Store listing fees are either $0.05 or $0.10 for 30 days, as opposed to the much higher auction listing fees. (See Appendix B for eBay's listing fees.)

Nathan has stressed customer service, quick shipping, and clear descriptions. He has made sure to provide his customers with every available opportunity to contact him directly by providing his e-mail address, telephone number, Skype name, instant messenger name, and more, in a way that is clear for customers to see. By displaying the company's contact information he gives customers the knowledge that they will have plenty of recourse should the sale not go as expected. This instills trust in his new customers who may not yet be familiar with the company's excellent service.

One-quarter of Blue Star's business now comes in through eBay. They are a PowerSeller with 99.9% positive feedback over 1,985 sales. They have earned their rank admirably and are a great example of how to effectively leverage eBay as a means to expand a business.

QUick pRofile

- Blue Star Computer Corporation
- 7 October Hill Road, Suite 4
- Holliston, MA 01746
- Telephone: 508-429-3001
- AOL Instant Messenger: bluestarcsr
- Skype: bluestarebay
- Web Site: www.bluestarusa.com
- eBay User ID: bluestarcomputersales
- eBay Store: www.stores.ebay.com/bluestarcomputercorp
- My World Page: http://myworld.ebay.com/bluestarcomputersales
- Company Description: Since 1994, Blue Star Computer Corporation has provided competitive advantage and measurable strategic value to customers. They achieve this customer value by supplying same-day shipping of quality new, refurbished, and proprietary spare computer hardware and components.

Getting Started

Your first steps in the world of eBay should be spent poking around and finding out all that the community has to offer. Getting to know the environment in which you're investing so much time and energy will only produce desirable results.

eBay has a wide variety of services to offer. Beyond the auctions and item listings, eBay is home to discussion boards, blogs, guides, specialty sites, and dozens of other services. In order to make the most of your time on eBay, you should become familiar enough with all of the services offered to know which ones you should using, and which of them you can do without.

Some of the extra services that eBay offers are available to anyone on the Internet, whether an eBay member or not. Their communication software, Skype, for example is available not only to eBay members, but to everybody in the world. The most high-profile nonexclusive service, of course, is their popular PayPal service. Some of eBay's specialty sites, such as Half.com and Shopping.com, are open to everybody as well. And even some of the eBay-specific tools, such as eBay Express and the Solutions Directory—both of which will be explained later—are open to all comers, whether registered on eBay or not.

In the above cases, you can explore these different services without an eBay ID. In all other cases, though, membership is required—and since you will need an eBay ID anyway, you should begin exploring eBay by registering for the site.

rEgistering

Becoming an eBay member is simple. eBay has made it a straightforward process involving some brief forms you must fill out. You do not register on eBay as a buyer *or* a seller, as is the case with many marketplace sites. Instead you register as a community member, capable of both buying and selling. The eBay ID (sometimes called username) you select during this process will become your eBay identity. Also, the feedback you earn with your new eBay ID will be for both your buying and selling activity. There is no distinction between feedback gained through buying or feedback gained through selling. A positive is a positive, regardless of which side of the transaction you were on.

When you first come to ebay.com, you will see a blue "register" link near the top of the page. Clicking this link will begin the registration process. While the process itself is easy, the answers you provide should be carefully thought out. The information you provide here will be difficult (and sometimes damaging) to change later.

User ID

During this process, you will be asked to select an eBay User ID. This is the name you will be assigning to your eBay identity. It will be how buyers and sellers come to know you. Selecting an appropriate eBay ID is important, so it must be done with great care—but it is also the most enjoyable part of the process.

Individual sellers have the luxury of creativity in this task. They can name themselves anything. For example, IDs like "bunnylover06," "ThorTheWarriorKing," or "ThisSiteIsTheGreatestThingEverYAAAY" all fit within eBay's User ID guidelines. As long as the crazily named user maintains a respectable feedback rating, buyers will buy their items.

hElpful hInt

For security and technological reasons, eBay dictates certain guidelines for User IDs by which every new registrant must abide. They are as follows:

User IDs:
- ☞ may contain letters (a–z), numbers (0–9), and/or some symbols
- ☞ must be at least two characters long
- ☞ can't contain spaces
- ☞ can't be obscene, profane, or violate eBay's guidelines
- ☞ can't be an e-mail address or web address (Note: Some users get around this.)
- ☞ can't be the same as another sellers' eBay Store name
- ☞ can't contain the @, &, ', <, or > symbols
- ☞ can't be URLs (example: xyz.com)
- ☞ can't contain consecutive underscores (__)
- ☞ can't have an underscore (_), hyphen (-)", or period (.) at the beginning of a User ID
- ☞ can't contain spaces or tabs
- ☞ can't contain the word "eBay" (only eBay employees may use "eBay" in their User IDs)
- ☞ can't be the letter "e" followed by numbers

For the most current eBay User ID policies, see:
http://pages.ebay.com/help/reg/contextual/createuserid.html.

You, I'm afraid, have more limitations. The eBay ID you select should reflect well on your business. In fact, it is a good idea, and my recommendation, that you use some variation on the existing the name of your business. Trumbull Mountain chose trumbullmtn. Blue Star chose bluestarcomputersales. Both were safe choices and reflected the original business well. Using your business's name gives your eBay ID an inherent professionalism that adds to your credibility with buyers right away.

If you choose not to use your company's name, select something appropriate for your product lines. For example, if you are a seller of tennis equipment, consider "TennisPro," "DiscountTennis," "TennisAuctions," and the like. An item-inappropriate eBay ID, like "ilove2skip," won't do much for your brand recognition.

After you select an eBay ID, you will be asked to provide some personal information, including a credit or debit card number. Registration on eBay is free. Your card will not be charged. eBay simply requires this information to make sure that everybody buying and selling on eBay is who they claim to be. In order for eBay to succeed, buyers and sellers must be able to trust each other. This is one precaution eBay takes to make sure that their marketplace remains a safe place to do business.

Once you have registered you will receive a few e-mails welcoming you to the community and inviting you to get started. Also, your browser will spit out a confirmation page. In order to begin selling on eBay you will need to provide them with a little more information. Click the link on the confirmation page to continue on eBay with selling privileges.

eBay will ask you for some financial information that will allow them to collect the selling fees you will be paying to list your items. Once this process is complete, you will be a full-fledged eBay buyer and seller.

eBay sTores

As mentioned briefly in the introduction, eBay launched a program called eBay Stores to help encourage businesses to sell their goods through eBay. Sellers who subscribe to the eBay Store program are given a customizable store on eBay—that is separate from all the other listings—in which they can stock and organize their items. Stores are given a unique and memorable URL to make it easy for customers to

†Rumbull's sTumbles

The web address that your eBay Store is assigned is a variation of the name you give to your eBay Store. For example, if your store is named "Linda's Linens," your eBay Store URL would be http://stores.ebay.com/Lindas-Linens.

When Trumbull Mountain first signed up for their eBay Store they assigned it the name "trumbullmtn" to reflect their external web address (www.trumbullmtn.com) and to give them the desirable store URL of http://stores.ebay.com/trumbullmtn. This tactic, they thought, would make it easy for their customers to visit their store and remember how to find it.

However, while this strategy worked for them in that one respect, it hurt them in another. In the eBay Stores directory, your store is listed exactly as you named it. So the Trumbull Mountain store showed up as simply "trumbullmtn." All of their competition in the category had chosen longer, more professional names for their stores, which showed up in the directory listing as "North Country Tack and Saddle," and "Green Valley Farm Saddlery." When displayed amongst these professional and conventional store names, the amalgamation "trumbullmtn" looked silly and unprofessional.

Trumbull Mountain chose to rename their store to "Trumbull Mountain Tack Shop." This gave them a more professional listing in the eBay Stores directory, but it also changed their store URL to **http://stores.ebay.com/Trumbull-Mountain-Tack-Shop**. This small change cost Trumbull Mountain a lot of frustration in editing their customized store pages, e-mail templates, and advertising in order to change the store address from the old to the new.

return. This is a great way to have a fully stocked, easy-to-manage, online store with the instant potential for millions of customers.

Visitors to your store will only see your products. These stores can be stocked with fixed-price listings for a fee of only $0.05 or $0.10 per item every 30 days. Large sellers, like Blue Star, use their eBay Store as their main method of selling online.

I suggest you sign up for an eBay Store right away for a number of reasons. First, every subscriber to eBay Stores is given a little storefront icon beside their eBay ID. Even if you have zero feedback, people who see this little icon beside your name will know that you're serious enough about selling on eBay that you're willing to shell out the monthly fee for an eBay Store. This provides you with some easy credibility right out of the gate.

Second, customizing an eBay Store takes some time. Before you stock it full of items, you should experiment with different layout, colors, and customization. Use this time while you're getting your store set up to begin buying on eBay. Buy something—anything. Participating in transactions will give you valuable insights into how the process works. Also, you will increase your feedback rating. Most buyers will not buy from someone with zero feedback, and therefore opening your fully stocked, fully customized store right now would do you little good. You need to get your feedback rating up before anybody will take you seriously. If you can't think of anything to buy, you can always purchase the shipping supplies you'll no doubt need once the sales begin rolling in.

> ## sTrategy sNippet
>
> Trumbull Mountain decided to replace the main page of their eBay Store with an entirely customized page. This benefits Trumbull Mountain in four main ways: it makes their eBay Store stand out from all the template-based versions of their competitors; it provides them an opportunity to pitch their higher-priced items, seasonal specials, and close-out deals; and it makes their off-eBay promotion of the store more effective by presenting visitors with an attractive and "non–eBay-formatted" page; and finally it gave Trumbull Mountain a distinct character that set it apart from other eBay sellers.

To sign up for an eBay Store, click on "My eBay," click "Subscriptions" under the My Account heading, and then scroll down to the eBay Stores section. Read about the three different levels of subscription, and select the one that is best for you. Once you have subscribed, you can begin to manage your store by clicking the My eBay tab, and then scrolling down to the Manage My Store link on the left side of the resulting page.

aBout mE

Every seller is offered the use of an About Me page. This is a partially customizable page that allows sellers to give buyers a profile of who they are. This is a free service provided as part of the eBay Community section. Not all sellers take advantage of their About Me page—though they should—most likely because it is difficult to figure out where to begin setting one up.

Many sellers spend a lot of time searching through the obvious places where it should be (My eBay, Sellers Preferences, Manage My Store, etc.). Instead, of wasting all that time, just follow these directions. Click "Community" on the top of eBay's main page, then scroll to the bottom of the resulting page and click the "Create an About Me page" link. Then click the "Create Your Page" button, and select the process through which you would like to create your page: templates or custom HTML.

This About Me page is the only place on eBay where you are allowed to post an off-eBay link, to your business web site for example. eBay prohibits sellers from inviting buyers they meet on eBay to conduct the transaction via a method that robs eBay of the fees it deserves.

Use your About Me page to provide your buyers with your business information. The most effective About Me pages provide buyers with the story of your business. Tell your buyers who you are, what makes you special, how long you've been in business, and what your goals are on eBay. Put up photos of your storefront, warehouse, or offices. If you can, persuade your employees to pose for a group photo. And don't forget to include the office pet. The combination of these elements will provide your buyers with the sense that you are a legitimate business run by actual people. This will make them feel good about sending you their hard-earned money.

mY wOrld

Similar to your About Me page is your My World page. Unlike your About Me page, your My World page does not allow for any HTML customization. It takes a more novice-friendly approach to helping users customize their pages by offering optional content widgets containing such information as recent feedback comments, eBay blog posts, active listings, a brief biography, and a photograph.

Many speculate that the My World service will ultimately replace the About Me page service. It seems to me that the My World community is eBay's attempt at setting up a user-content-driven community such as MySpace, Friendster, and Facebook. There is also a suspiciously large white space along the right side of the My World pages. The purpose of this space becomes more clear when seen in the light of the recent deal between eBay and Google. Be on the lookout for Google-generated and eBay-specific ads here in the not-so-distant-future.

In terms of your own selling, your My World page just gives you one more place to provide information about your business and your items. It is worthwhile to customize, but don't spend too much energy here.

m^Y eBay

At the top of most eBay pages you will see a link to your My eBay page. This page is your eBay "control panel" or "dashboard" as the trendy folks are calling it now. On this page you will find information about all your eBay goings-on: the items you're selling, the items you're buying, the items you're watching, your sold items, your unsold items, and so on. This is also the page from which you will control all of your eBay settings and preferences.

Down the left side of the page are links to various settings and services. You should take time to explore each of the different options available to you. Links of note in this column include the Personal Information link, the Preferences link, and the Subscriptions link. These links are the meat of this page during set-up and should help you get things organized and underway.

If you have subscribed to the eBay Stores program, they likely tossed in a free subscription to their management tool Selling Manager Pro. (This is a "temporary" promotion that I've never seen them not offer.) If this is the case, the Selling Manager Pro tools will replace your My eBay tools after clicking the My eBay link. I cover Selling Manager Pro in more detail in the Chapter 9, Listing Management. To return to your basic, original My eBay tools, you will need to click the View My eBay Selling link at the bottom of the left-hand column in Selling Manager Pro.

c^Ommunity b^Oards

The Community Boards serve as eBay's center. This is where thousands (if not millions) of eBay users meet every day for a free exchange of advice, strategies, and ideas. You could learn a lot very quickly about eBay by becoming an active participant in these discussion boards.

If you ever find yourself baffled by any aspect of eBay, the Community Boards are a great place to turn. With so many experienced eBay users crowded onto these boards, you're likely to get a quick and helpful answer to any questions you post. You'll find that eBay members, particularly those that participate in these discussions, are wonderfully generous with their assistance to new members of the community.

The boards are also a popular hangout for many eBay employees, so the company itself is very aware of the discussions taking place. If you have a bone to pick with eBay about one issue or another, starting a discussion topic about it on the boards is a good way to make your gripes heard. And, with so many sellers in the community, it is likely that if you have a gripe, thousands of others have a similar gripe and will join you in sounding off about the problem.

I don't want to give you the impression that the Community Boards exist to give eBay a hard time. They exist to help eBay users meet each other and therefore strengthen the community as a whole. On the boards it is entirely possible to meet 10 people from 6 different countries—all with similar interests—every day. It truly is a collection of users from around the world.

sOme eBay tOols

eBay provides many tools for both buyers and sellers. Navigating the huge eBay landscape can be difficult and confusing. It is of course in eBay's interest to make their service as easy to use as possible, and to that end, the company publishes the following services that aim to make eBay easier to navigate.

Solutions Directory

One of the greatest resources for members that eBay has put together is the Solutions Directory. This directory is the best way to find eBay management tools from both eBay and third-party software publishers. Buyers and sellers can find programs and services that help them manage everything from auction listings to inventory to their photographs.

The directory is split into three main categories: buying, selling, and other. Within the selling category you can browse for programs to help you with listing, inventory, e-mails, checkout, and much more. There are thousands of offerings, each with a rating and brief description.

eBay has blessed some programs and services with its approval. These offerings are tagged with an "eBay Certified Provider" image. I recommend you stick with eBay certified providers, as there a many available from which to choose and they are guaranteed to offer a quality service.

Marketplace Research

Sellers should know whether or not the items they intend to list on eBay are selling well on the site, or not at all. The standard method for researching an item's sales record is to use eBay's advanced search to find the recent completed listings for that item. This method will give you a general idea as to whether the item is in demand or not.

However, most sellers would like to have more than a general idea about the item's selling trends, and therefore eBay launched their Marketplace Research tool. This research tool will provide sellers with more specific sales information for particular keywords such as average sale price, average bids per item, average starting price, and so on. This sort of information will help you make a more informed decision about how, and when, and whether or not, to list items.

There are many such research tools available beyond eBay's. In fact, eBay's Marketplace Research, even at the highest subscription level, has been criticized as being scant on really useful information.

> **hElpful hInt**
>
> I recommend you first explore the services from Andale, Terapeak, and HammerTap at the web sites below.
> - Andale: www.andale.com
> - Terapeak: www.terapeak.com
> - HammerTap: www.hammertap.com
>
> Each has been highly recommended by eBay sellers for many years, and each has been in existence long before eBay's Marketplace Research service.

Explore the Solutions Directory for other research services before deciding on just one.

eBay Pulse

eBay Pulse is as much for buyers as it is for sellers. Located at **http://pulse.ebay.com**, it is a simple tool that brings together all the popularity information for items all across eBay and presents a blurb about the most popular items in the most popular categories. Sometimes it will display an article about a particular item or category, but it is mostly filled with superficial information. Think of it as the tabloid aisle of eBay.

It's useful only to discover the largest trends occurring on eBay, but beyond that, it won't do sellers much good.

eBay Pop

eBay Pop, located at **http://pages.ebay.com/ebaypop/**, is a summary of all the popular culture items selling on eBay. Think of it as the teen magazine of eBay. It lists the top 10 best-selling and fastest-accelerating DVDs, fashion items, tech gadgets, CDs, and such. You can learn about the pop "Item of the Week," and various popular-culture-related stories concerning items on eBay.

This site is useful to check in on once in a while, but by no means should you depend on Pop as a viable means for research.

Reviews and Guides

The Reviews and Guides link on the left side of eBay's main page will take you to a peculiar section of eBay. In eBay's ongoing attempt to create and expand as a community, they have created a tool that allows community members to review items (movies, games, cameras, etc.) and to write guides on any topic (how to keep leather clean, how to choose running shoes, how to select a timeshare, etc.). You can browse both the reviews and guides by category.

I Want It Now

The Want It Now tool is designed to help connect buyers and sellers. Buyers who cannot find the item for which they're searching can post an item request to the Want It Now directory. Sellers who are seeking new products to sell can browse the postings in this directory to see what is in demand—at least by one person.

If you have a basement or warehouse full of oddities and you're unsure what to begin selling, browse through the Want It Now directory for an idea where to begin.

Wholesale

The eBay Wholesale directory is a section of eBay dedicated to buying and selling items in bulk. This is a particularly useful section for sellers to know about as it can be a great place to find more products to sell, more shipping materials in bulk, and other business supplies by the pallet. Need a truckload of foam peanuts? Search here.

Blogs

eBay is trying to leave community members with no reason to leave the eBay universe. Popular services such as MySpace, Blogger, and Amazon are being copied into eBay with services like My World, eBay Blogs, and eBay Express—each with varying degrees of success.

For sellers interested in making eBay their world, these services hold value. For most businesses looking to expand to eBay, these services are just noise in the background. Small business owners have enough to do without worrying about participating in quarrels on the eBay blogs about who sold what first and for how much.

Unless you can find an inventive use for these blogs, I don't expect they'll do much to help you with your sales. (Blogging for your business, in general, can be quite beneficial to your sales if done properly. These eBay Blogs are a long way from "done properly" in terms of business blogging.)

sPecialty sItes

eBay expands its range of services every year. Often these expansions take the form of what they call "specialty sites." These sites are themed sections of eBay's selling platform. For example, when the Cars, Boats, Vehicles, and Parts category grew to enormous portions, eBay expanded it into the eBay Motors specialty site. When eBay decided to focus on selling to business customers, they created the eBay Business specialty site. Below are some of the latest additions to the specialty site roster.

eBay Express

After conducting years of research about buyer behavior, eBay decided that it was missing out on a huge market of convenience buyers. These are the shoppers who would prefer to use a drive-through than to go into the store. There are many choices to be made when shopping on eBay: auction or Buy It Now, eBay Store or fixed-price listing, do I trust this seller or not? Often, for tired or worn-out shoppers, this is more mental energy than they care to expend before falling into bed.

To meet the needs of these convenience shoppers (and to compete with sites like Amazon.com, Newegg.com, and HomeDepot.com) eBay created eBay Express. Items from sellers' fixed-price listings and eBay Store items are listed automatically in eBay Express. Buyers can search for and purchase any of these items, and expect that the item will ship right away—instead of when the auction ends.

hElpful hInt

In order for items to be automatically included in eBay Express, the seller of the items must:

- maintain a feedback score of 100 or more, 98% positive or better
- maintain a public feedback profile
- support your listings with a PayPal Premier or PayPal Business account
- ensure your PayPal account settings are set to ship to unconfirmed addresses or make sale-by-sale decisions ("Ask me for unconfirmed addresses")
- be registered as a U.S. registered seller, or Canadian registered seller shipping from the U.S.

And the items must:

- be listed on eBay.com
- be listed in Fixed Price, Store Inventory, or Auction-style with Buy It Now format
- have a completed item condition field (i.e. New, Used, Refurbished) in Item Specifics, using the predefined values (some categories exempted)
- use Pre-Filled Item Information for listings within Books, DVDs & Movies, Music, & Video Games
- include shipping costs (flat, calculated, or free) in the shipping fields.

☞ provide a picture
☞ allow shoppers to pay by single, combined payments for their purchases. You can specify this by going to your Selling Preferences
  within My eBay. Look for the Shipping & Discount section.
☞ offer eBay checkout or the new checkout integration API (for 3rd
  party order processing)
☞ be located in the United States
☞ not exceed $10,000.00 in price

eBay Motors

As mentioned above, eBay created eBay Motors to handle all their automotive-related products. This accomplished two things: it separated the huge automotive traffic out of eBay.com; and it gave the automotive shoppers better automotive-specific service.

If you are looking to sell on eBay Motors, you will be happy to know that the site operates very similarly to the plain old eBay.com. However, there are some differences (such as higher fees), and you will benefit from poking around before you get started.

eBay Stores

The eBay Stores specialty site is simply the searchable directory of eBay Stores. Buyers can search through the directory for items, names of sellers, and names of the individual stores. This site, in all likelihood, was eBay's attempt at what ultimately became eBay Express.

If you have subscribed to the eBay Stores program, your site will be listed here. If you subscribed to the Featured level of subscription, your store will be listed in one of the Featured boxes, along with your logo, at the top of the appropriate category page, in rotating order. Anchor stores are shown on the directory's main page, in rotating order.

eBay Business

For calculators, PDAs, pens, paper, staples, printers, computers, chairs, desks, and whatever else you would need in your office, eBay has built eBay Business. This site, like eBay Motors, is simply eBay with a slant toward a particular item genre.

If you're in the office products industry, you will find that eBay Business is a place where you'll be spending a lot of time. For sellers of all other types of items, this is a great place to shop for your business needs.

sIte mAp

The eBay Site Map link is at the bottom of most of eBay's main pages. This ever-evolving page will sum up for you eBay's expansive universe. As a seller you will often become so wrapped up in your own business that you'll be unaware of new eBay services or sites. Therefore, it is a good move to check the eBay Site Map occasionally to check up on the latest additions. Some of what you've missed could very well be incredibly helpful to your business.

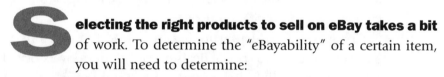

eChapter three

Selecting Products

Selecting the right products to sell on eBay takes a bit of work. To determine the "eBayability" of a certain item, you will need to determine:

- the item's average success rate on eBay,
- whether or not you can reorder the item reliably,
- whether or not you can buy the item at a low enough cost,
- whether or not the item is easily delivered to the buyers.

To minimize risk when expanding to eBay, it is best to base your eBay sales on items that you know to sell well, can be sold profitably, and can be reliably received by the customer. Any snags in the early days of selling on eBay can sap your sales rate for a long time. For example, if you sell four items on your first day and find that you can't—for whatever reason—ship two of them, you might come up with two positive and two negative feedback ratings very quickly. A 50% positive feedback rating will destroy your chances of selling on eBay. Buyers will avoid your items like the plague. You might need to start entirely over under a new user ID. Reliability for your business translates to reliability for your customer.

As an established business, you have several advantages over eBay start-ups. You already have established supplier relationships and a steady stream of inventory into your business. You can order and reorder items in half the time it would take a new business to do the researching, calling around, product selection, and ordering. This will help you get items to customers reliably.

Also, you have a knowledge of your industry and its biggest players: sellers, suppliers, distributors, and so on. Knowing the right people to contact when hunting down the best prices for the best-selling items will be a huge advantage when trying to improve profitability.

Finally, your "in" with suppliers may lead to better prices for the items you order, or to special deals on close-out or overstocked items.

This chapter will walk you through the steps of selecting products to sell on eBay. So grab your inventory list and a few catalogs from your suppliers. Have them, and a highlighter, handy while you read through this chapter and mark items that come to mind as you read. By the end of this chapter you should have a good idea of several items that you can list right away.

yOur cUrrent iNventory

The first place to begin searching for "eBayable" items is from within your own existing inventory. Since you are likely anxious to begin selling on eBay, there are no items that you'll be able to photograph, describe, and ship faster than the ones sitting around your warehouse or showroom.

Old Inventory

Your earliest goal for selling on eBay is to build a positive feedback rating. Buying items on eBay in the first few weeks will help you get some green on your feedback page. However, if you're looking to sell items, it is best to earn some positive feedback from eBay buyers. Often buyers will check to see how a seller has earned their feedback rating, through buying or selling. If the buyer sees that a seller is offering the $5,000 item in which he's interested, but the seller has never sold anything on eBay before, the buyer will likely move on.

So, after bringing your feedback rating up to about 10—and earning your first star—you should try your hand at selling low-cost items that are related to your most expensive products. For example, Trumbull Mountain earned a 100% positive feedback rating of 5 by buying some office supplies on eBay. This gave them the basic foundation they needed to begin selling. Then, Edie began cleaning out the back room, which, over the years, had collected bridles, horse blankets, riding boots, and such, that hadn't sold for years. These were perfectly good—new and used—items, that for some reason just didn't sell. Trumbull

eBay's Feedback Star System

Feedback points are awarded in the following manner:

1. +1 point to your feedback score for each positive comment and rating left for you
2. 0 points to your feedback score for each neutral comment and rating left for you
3. −1 point to your feedback score for each negative comment and rating left for you

Once you receive 10 feedback points you are awarded your first star. As your points increase, the star you are awarded changes to reflect your growing success. These stars are displayed as a badge of pride by both buyers and sellers.

Here's what the different stars mean:

☞ Yellow Star = 10 to 49 points
☞ Blue Star = 50 to 99 points
☞ Turquoise Star = 100 to 499 points
☞ Purple Star = 500 to 999 points
☞ Red Star = 1,000 to 4,999 points
☞ Green Star = 5,000 to 9,999 points
☞ Yellow Shooting Star = 10,000 to 24,999 points
☞ Turquoise Shooting Star = 25,000 to 49,999 points
☞ Purple Shooting Star = 50,000 to 99,999 points
☞ Red Shooting Star = 100,000 or higher

Mountain used eBay as an outlet for these items that wasted space in their already cramped store, and tied up a lot money they could use to buy items that would sell more reliably. They listed it all on eBay.

Most of the items were placed at auction using the One Dollar-No Reserve ($1NR) strategy to guarantee that they would sell and could therefore be cleaned out of the back room. (See Chapter 9, Listing Management, for more about $1NR.) Edie didn't expect to get much out of the pile of items and was just happy to reclaim some of the money that these items represented. All of the old inventory did sell. Some items, such as a pair of custom fitted men's riding boots, sold for far more than anyone at Trumbull Mountain expected. But most of it sold for just a few dollars.

As a result of selling off the dead stock and old inventory, Trumbull Mountain cleaned out their back room (which they made into the eBay sales office and photography studio), added to their cash flow, and, most importantly, achieved a 100% positive feedback rating of 51—earning them their first yellow, and then blue, feedback stars.

With these two stars under their belt, they had now established a credible feedback rating and could therefore begin to list the more expensive items in their inventory.

Attack your piles of dead stock, clean out your storerooms, and sell off everything that hasn't sold. Don't expect this strategy to be profitable; consider it to be the price of establishing a quick and positive feedback rating, which will lead to more profitable sales.

> ### sTrategy sNippet
>
> When selling off your old items, be sure to describe them accurately. If they are used, or otherwise imperfect, say so in your description and display the flaws in your photographs. These first few sales are not intended to bring in money. They are intended to bring in positive feedback. Therefore, the more accurately you can describe these items—even if they're heinous, beaten, or downright broken—the better.

New Inventory

Selling your current and up-to-date inventory can be a good deal trickier than selling your older stuff. Anything is "eBayable" if it's priced low enough. But selling your main inventory, profitably, takes some more finesse. There are many factors to consider; the most important of all is, of course, profitability.

Before you list any of your new items for sale on eBay, you must be sure that doing so does not violate any agreements you've made with your suppliers. Many manufacturers and distributors forbid their sellers from selling on any auction sites, especially eBay. This may seem like an unfair restriction to impose on their sellers—after all you did buy the items outright—but in actuality this is a measure taken to protect their sellers from price erosion. If one renegade seller of saddles begins listing new saddles on eBay at auction, that seller can't guarantee the final selling price of that saddle. Therefore, they could very well end up undercutting the sale price offered by, and agreed to by, the other sellers. If buyers can get the saddle for significantly cheaper at auction, why would they buy anywhere else?

For this reason, eBay still carries a severely negative connotation for many suppliers, who will justifiably cancel agreements with sellers who undercut their other sellers. So, to protect your supply lines, and to remain in good standing with your suppliers, be sure that selling on eBay is not forbidden in your agreement. If it's allowed, feel free to sell away. If it's forbidden, there are some steps you can take.

Suppliers fear eBay because the auction selling format removes the price control mechanisms on which they rely. It robs them of their ability to guarantee a profitably selling item to their retailers. However, what you already know (and what they don't) is that eBay has expanded beyond the purely auction selling format with which it launched. eBay sellers can guarantee selling prices in a variety of ways. eBay is not the problem, selling at auction is the problem, and there are many ways around that. If a manufacturer has forbidden you from selling on eBay, try explaining to them that eBay is no longer solely an auction site. Sellers can list these items in a customized eBay Store where prices are fixed and guaranteed. In this way, an eBay Store is no different than selling in any other online store. Also, request that they change their agreement's wording to forbid sellers from selling below a certain price, not from selling on eBay and other emerging marketplaces altogether.

Once you've established which items you're allowed to sell and which you are not, you should begin to judge the permissible items' eBayability. This is determined by three main factors: selling rate, selling price, and ease of delivery. Each can be quantified by the appropriate tools, some of which we cover below. It is important to determine the eBayability of each item before you invest in more inventory, invest in the proper shipping materials, and even invest in time spent photographing and describing your items. There is no point to spending time with an item if it has proven impossible to sell through eBay.

The first place to check out whether or not an item will sell on eBay is in eBay's own forbidden items list. If eBay won't sell it, neither will you. This list is quite long, always expanding, and contains some seemingly innocuous items that you might not expect to find there, like postage meters, textbooks, gift cards, and consumables. For the complete and current list, go to **http://pages.ebay.com/help/policies/items-ov.html**.

Ease of shipping is also a consideration. For example, if you find that you can sell cast iron wood-burning stoves profitably at $100 off the normal retail price, but your buyers will need to pay $101 for shipping, then you've lost your advantage. It will be cheaper for your customers to pay retail locally and borrow a pick-up truck from their brother-in-law. Buyers always factor shipping expenses into the item's final price. Be careful that the items you sell don't end up being more expensive than your customers' local options.

This takes us to one of the largest ongoing tasks of any eBay seller: item research. There are a few methods for tackling item research. Blue Star, for example, does research for every item it lists every day. Before listing any new item they haven't sold on eBay before, they conduct a significant investigation into the item's sales history on eBay. They've become so familiar with the process and tools necessary to do this that the whole process can take only five to ten minutes.

Trumbull Mountain, on the other hand, does research less often. Instead of conducting research every day, they reevaluate their entire eBay product line every month or so. This method saves them time in their daily activities and refreshes their eBay listings with highly eBayable items every month. It runs the risk of costing them more time than it would Blue Star to investigate an entire inventory, but with their own sales records from previous months, they have a good idea at the beginning of the process which items need to be swapped out.

You should devise and refine your own strategy for researching your eBay product line. But no matter at what point, and on what schedule, you decide to do your research you will find the following tools helpful.

Completed Listings. The quick and dirty strategy for researching items is to use eBay's Advanced Search tool to browse the recently completed listings for a particular item. "Recently" is used loosely here because eBay tends to change the amount of time into the past it chooses to display for completed listings. At one time eBay displayed a month of listings, then only two weeks. Currently it is displaying three weeks of data. By clicking the Advanced Search link to the right of eBay's main search box, you will be presented with a host of additional search options. For our present purposes, you need only to click the checkbox next to "Completed listings only" underneath the text box. Enter a keyword or item model number into the text field and click "Search."

In the resulting list you will see all the recently sold (prices in green) and unsold (prices in red) items. By glancing down along the red and green numbers you will be able to glean a rough estimate for the demand that exists on eBay for that particular item. If you see mostly green, then the market could stand some more of that same item. If you see mostly red, then, unless you can sell the item for significantly less than everybody else, it's probably best to move on.

This list of completed items will also display the number of bids that each item received. If most of the items that ended up selling successfully received a few dozen bids or more, you've stumbled onto a popular item. If the bids are low across the board, interest is as well.

For those of you who would like more than quick and dirty data on which to base your products decisions, you'll be happy to know that the existence of eBay has launched an industry committed to eBay research.

Marketplace Research. In order to capitalize on the cottage eBay research industry that was emerging, eBay created its own service called Marketplace Research.

Marketplace Research is a simple tool that allows you to search completed listings, just as outlined above, but instead of 20 or so days of data, you are given access to the previous 90. Also, the information you are given about the last 90 days of completed listings is much more extensive than what a simple completed listings search produces. For example, you can see average sale prices, percentage of successful sales, average shipping cost per item, and through which platform the item sold (auction, fixed-price, Buy It Now, eBay Stores, etc.).

eBay offers three subscription levels. You can subscribe to this service through your subscriptions manager on your My eBay page. Visit **http://pages.ebay.com/marketplace_research** to learn more.

Andale. Andale is one of the oldest and largest eBay research companies on the Internet. They launched in 1999 with simple visitor counters for sellers' auction pages and have been offering tools for sellers every since.

Andale's research tool is widely seen as the best available. It is also among the least expensive. Andale can tell you nearly everything you need to know about your items and how they're selling on eBay: average sale price, the best time to list, the best days to end an auction, the best way to sell for the highest price, and more. For only $7.95 per month, this is a tool you should use at least once if for nothing more than to test its usefulness for yourself.

Andale understands the information necessary to make good eBay decisions. And they present that information in a clear, readable format. Find out more at **http://www.andale.com.**

Terapeak. Terapeak offers a research service that is similar to those above. Terapeak has been around a long time as well, comes highly recommended, and, at the present time, is the only service to offer research of listings on eBay Motors—though their research is limited to parts and accessories. Terapeak has designed its interface to closely mimic the eBay site interface for familiar navigation. Terapeak offers several levels of service, and begins at only $9.95 per month.

HammerTap. HammerTap offers a range of seller services in addition to their eBay research tool, Deep Analysis. This is the most expensive service at $24.95 per month. The only reason I can see for the price difference is that HammerTap tosses in their FeeFinder and BidderBlocker tools when you purchase the research program. FeeFinder calculates your eBay fees for you before you submit your listing, and BidderBlocker prevents unwanted bidders (that you specify) from submitting bids on your items. I find both of these tools to be quite useful but available at no cost from other companies.

nEw sOurces

eBay has come a long way from its bargain basement beginnings. People are now more willing than ever to pony up retail prices for items bought on eBay, but that doesn't mean that great bargains don't sell faster. The key to selling profitably while still offering great bargains is not to violate your sales agreements. Another key, to avoid taking a huge hit against your profits, is to buy cheap. Cheaper than cheap. And a great place to find new, cheap, inventory, oddly enough, is directly from your existing suppliers.

Just as you had a large pile of unsold stock, your suppliers may have warehouses full of costly, slow-moving merchandise. Luckily for them, and for you, eBay is a great way to clean out those warehouses. The next time you speak to your suppliers, ask them if they have any dead stock that they would like to liquidate. More often than not they are happy to turn those piles (or warehouses) of slow-moving merchandise into fast cash. They regain their inventory space for new merchandise, and you can buy items at great deals—sometimes for pennies on the dollar.

For years Trumbull Mountain received the occasional informal "Hey, we're discounting this stuff" e-mail from one of their main suppliers. They took no notice of it because the stuff that sold slowly for their supplier would also sell slowly in their showroom. But eBay presented a new opportunity. Trumbull Mountain contacted that supplier and learned that not only did they have the dead stock from the most recent e-mail, but they had mountains more. After some quick research on eBay, Trumbull submitted an order for perfectly good, but underperforming, items from this supplier. It arrived, and because Trumbull Mountain had acquired it so cheaply, they were able to sell it fast and profitably on eBay. From that point on, Trumbull Mountain made a point to ask each of their suppliers about their availability of dead stock.

Another great place to find new items is on the Internet. Many product sourcing services have sprung up to serve the eBay seller community. One such service, Worldwide Brands, was started by eBay aficionado Chris Malta, specifically to meet the needs of online auction sellers who needed a place to find cheap and reliable sources for items.

hElpful hInt

Well-known shopping sites such as craigslist.org, shopping.com, honesty.com, and even eBay itself can provide you with great items to resell as well. Needless to say, finding the time to scour all of these sources for appropriate items at low enough prices is impossible given the time constraints of a small business. The good news is that all of these services, and thousands like them, provide RSS or Atom feeds that can make your job of searching these sites infinitely easier.

The best way to go about making use of these feeds is to download or purchase a feed reader program. These programs subscribe to the RSS or Atom feeds that are automatically published by these various shopping sites and alert you when there is an update to that feed. You can create customized feeds using a site's search function so that you are only alerted when an item of interest is posted to a site. For example, eBay offers RSS feeds for any search conducted on its site. Go to eBay and search for an item you would like to sell. At the bottom of the search listings you will find an orange RSS button link. By clicking this link you can subscribe to these search results with your feed reader. At an interval you specify, your feed reader will check these search results for you and alert you of any changes. You can use eBay's advanced search options to narrow your search down so that you're only alerted for highly popular items with prices that would allow you to sell for a profit. Everything else slides by.

This technique will work for all sites that offer both search functions and RSS feeds for the search results. Subscribing to search results feeds from classified advertisement sites, such as craigslist.org, may yield more profitable results for you since eBay's open marketplace tends to regulate prices—whereas sellers posting to classified ads sometimes simply guess the value of their goods.

A screenshot of a feed reader subscribed to the search results for the search term "1.25 mac mini" for 14 different cities on craigslist.org (See second screenshot on next page as well.)

In addition to new items from sources or suppliers, your customer returns are a great eBay profit source. As you know if you deal with a lot of customer returns, often diagnosing, fixing, and restocking the troubled item can be a costly and time-consuming endeavor. In fact, many large retailers such as Best Buy and Circuit City find it's cheaper just to destroy or recycle all of their customer returns whether they've been returned as damaged, faulty, or simply unwanted gifts.

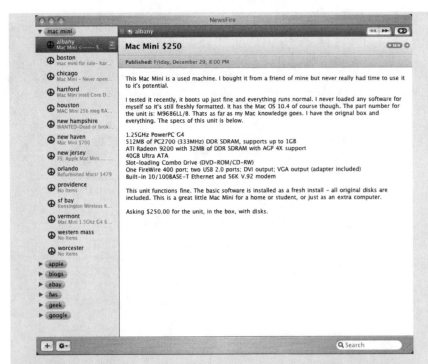

A screenshot of the content of an entry from craigslist.org detailing the product information and attractive selling price of this Mac mini. If you knew that the average selling price for this item is nearly $500 on eBay, this could be a lucrative automatic announcement for you.

Instead of wasting stock, you should give eBay a try. It is important that you do not sell these items as new. Once they leave your showroom, there's no telling what these items have been through. MP3 players may have been opened, computers may have been formatted, saddles may have been scuffed. Listing these items as used will ensure that your customers are not expecting a pristine item to arrive in the mail. Selling used items also carries some advantages: used items sell more quickly on eBay; and if your suppliers have a policy against selling their new merchandise on eBay, this is a good tack around it. "Like New" items are not new.

For years, Trumbull Mountain has offered a one-week trial-ride policy for each of its saddles. Because getting the properly fitting saddle for horse and rider is so important, Trumbull Mountain customers are encouraged to take home a brand new saddle, and, as Edie says, "Ride the sh*t out of it." If, after a week, the customer finds that the saddle doesn't fit well for any reason they can send it back for a full refund. This practice ensures that Trumbull Mountain has a steady stream of happy customers, and "demo" saddles. Edie estimates that only 25% of the time does a saddle remain sold after the first demo period—which proves that saddle fitting is a delicate art that Trumbull Mountain fully appreciates.

These demo saddles could be a problem for many saddle dealers when previously unowned saddles begin to show signs of wearing from multiple trial periods. (Not that many other saddle dealers offer a trial period at all—and Trumbull Mountain was the first and only for many years.) But as used and discounted items sell much faster and more reliably on eBay, Trumbull Mountain simply turns what could be a liability into an asset. They have a system in place that simultaneously provides unmatched customer service and improves the eBayability of their saddles.

Always be on the lookout for more product opportunities in your category. You never know from where the next great deal will spring. I'll share one more story with you, and then move on to the next chapter. In conducting research for one of my other eBay books, I met a seller, John, who didn't start from an established business, but instead left his job—in spite of the doubts expressed by his family and friends—to pursue selling full-time on eBay.

John was a computer hobbyist. He liked to spend his time building, refining, and perfecting his home-built computer systems. He admitted to me that he had a stack of CDs in his office of 30 different operating systems from around the globe and he would often try to put them all on one machine. When these machines he built would get a little long in the tooth, he would disassemble them and sell them for parts. He learned over time that there was a good market for second-generation computer components on eBay. His items always sold reliably and he made a decent profit on most things. And since John had been building computers for years, he also knew the cheapest places to find parts—or so he thought.

After leaving his job to sell full-time on eBay, John found that "the cheapest places to get parts" weren't that cheap at all. The profits that seemed adequate to him as a hobby seller weren't cutting it when he needed to depend on them for income. John decided that the only way to make this business work was to sell in massive quantities—something he didn't have the help or resources to do. After three disappointing months of selling on eBay, John had resigned himself to giving up.

The following Saturday John happened to stop in at a yard sale of a neighbor, Leonard, whom he had never met. John came across a box full of second-generation computer components just like he has been selling on eBay. Leonard was willing to let the whole box go for $20—an amount John knew he could quadruple easily. After discussing the components with Leonard, the discussion turned to John's hobby and struggling eBay business. Leonard became very excited and stunned John with the statement, "I have a warehouse full if you want it!"

It turned out that Leonard owned a small corporate computer leasing company and had, over the years, ended up with a warehouse of second-generation systems that were just taking up space. Leonard and John struck a deal that day, and John got immediately to work liquidating all of Leonard's old inventory. John's business took off.

This story gets right to my two points: you never know what's sitting just down the street; and it never hurts to ask.

eChapter fOur

Inventory

One of the largest decisions you will make at the beginning of this process is how to deal with the integration of your eBay inventory. Items being sold on eBay present some unique challenges for inventory. The auction process can make your items unavailable to sell through other channels for up to 10 days—and at the end of the 10 days, that item may not have sold at all, requiring you to restock it. Also, you may have some eBay items that aren't yet listed on the site and are therefore unavailable to eBay buyers. Do you make that inventory available in your showroom, or is it just stock that can't be sold? These are questions that must be addressed.

Before you start selling on eBay in earnest, you must have in place a system of managing both your eBay and regular inventories to ensure that items are always available for sale somewhere. However, this system must also ensure that items are not sold twice, lost between inventories, or incorrectly shipped. Inventory management is one of the largest challenges for businesses expanding to eBay because there is no one-size-fits-all solution. Your business has a unique setup and will require a unique solution. In this chapter I've detailed how some businesses manage this integration. These examples may work for you as they are explained, but more likely you will need to tweak them somewhat to shoehorn them into your business. For example, retail shops with a showroom will have different needs than mail-order businesses with just a warehouse. Stores with multiple locations will need to decide from which location to manage eBay sales and hold inventory.

There are several ways to go about inventory integration, and the method you choose (or invent) should be the one that simplifies (or doesn't complicate) your inventory process. The addition of eBay sales and stock should integrate seamlessly into your existing process. If your inventory management method becomes more complicated by adding eBay sales, you will lose efficiency, add expense, and weigh down your business. That is not the desired effect of expansion to any market.

This chapter will walk you through some of the most common solutions that have succeeded—and failed—for expanding businesses.

tWo iNventories

The first method of managing eBay inventory is to separate your eBay inventory out completely from the inventory you've dedicated to other sales channels. This will require dedicating separate physical space for your eBay stock, removing the items from your inventory manager program, and managing your eBay stock through other, independent means.

This may sound troublesome, but there are many benefits to this method. First, by separating your inventories completely, your eBay sales department can function as its own unit with its own autonomy. This will give your eBay sales team the flexibility they need to order only the items that are selling well on eBay, to sell any item they order at any time, and to simply dump the profits back into your main business at the end of every month. With enough staff, enough space, and reliable managers, this is a useful solution.

To make this solution work for your business, you will need certain tools to set up an independent eBay department. First, you will need to use an eBay inventory manager. There are many eBay-specific inventory managers available. These programs deal with the specific eccentricities of selling on eBay and aren't suitable to use for your regular inventory management. Some of these solutions are web-based, allowing you to set up your eBay inventory anywhere that you have space and an Internet connection, without sacrificing access to it from your main office.

The eBay Solutions Directory has a category devoted to eBay inventory management, which will guide you to some robust solutions. The businesses with which we spoke had mixed results with some of the programs they found in the directory, and a few even decided it was worth it to design their own eBay inventory management software.

Of the most popular choices for inventory management, eBay's Turbolister is always well-rated. ChannelAdvisor Pro's inventory manager is frustrating and hard to comprehend at times. And Kyozou's solution fares extremely well for larger eBay operations. I suggest you select an inventory manager that charges a flat monthly fee, instead of an incremental per-sale or per-item fee. The last thing you want your eBay inventory manager to do is discourage growth.

Smaller operations have found that a simple spreadsheet is enough to manage their eBay inventory. Microsoft Excel is the obvious choice for creating an inventory spreadsheet, but if you wanted more flexibility you might consider giving Google's spreadsheet service a try. This service allows you to access your spreadsheet from anywhere, giving you the freedom to work from another location without needing to worry about duplicate files with different information. If you don't have Excel, and don't want to spend the hundreds of dollars to acquire it, check out the OpenOffice.org suite of office applications. OpenOffice.org produces a full suite of office applications and distributes it for free as open-source software. See **www.openoffice.org** for more.

In addition to inventory management, you will need to work out an acceptable accounting method for your eBay department. Unfortunately, many eBay-specific solutions do not offer the level of financial reporting to which you're accustomed. As a business owner you understand the importance of reviewing the numbers. The sad fact is that the numbers and statistics provided by eBay's Selling

Manager Pro and eBay's Sales Reports can be hard to use and woefully light on information.

If your eBay management program doesn't provide you with adequate accounting tools—as many do not—the best place to find sales numbers is through eBay's Reporting link on the left side of your main Selling Manager Pro page. Here you will find monthly reports showing you the final sale price, the various fees, and the shipping costs associated with each sale. These numbers cannot be exported in any meaningful way.

The eBay Sales Reports tool is a free subscription accessed through your Subscriptions box on the left side of Selling Manager Pro. Though the title of this utility sounds promising, it is a joke and not worth the free subscription. Information for your monthly sales shows up between 6 to 8 weeks after the sales take place. The information displayed is half-complete, and the half they do show you is only mildly interesting. In my opinion eBay is embarrassing itself by offering this service and should either get it right or do away with it. Don't waste your time on it.

Finding a suitable accounting solution when using the two-inventory method will be difficult, and this is the main challenge of this method. However, the benefits of separating out your eBay inventory are tangible. Buying trends on eBay evolve more quickly than in conventional marketplaces. For example, Dell computer equipment that is selling like gangbusters on eBay one week may be followed up by six weeks of no interest because the market demand was satisfied after one week. This can be very frustrating for stores that have a warehouse full of Dell computer equipment.

By creating an autonomous eBay department you are able to follow the eBay trends more closely. If you find in your research that a specific type of item in your category is beginning to sell quickly, you won't have to restock your showroom's product line to suit the whimsy of eBay buyers. You need only to order the popular items for eBay and keep your usual inventory as it is.

When a business has multiple sales channels, but one inventory, the risk of selling one item twice can be significant. It is quite conceivable that if you've listed all the items in your store on eBay, one item could sell both from your store and on eBay. This creates a problem for you, particularly with unique items. The two-inventory method eliminates this risk.

The final benefit of using two inventories is that items placed at auction do not need to be taken out of your showroom or separated out of other salable inventory for days at a time. It is possible to end an auction early if the item sells through another sales channel. However, this practice is not recommended. Buyers expect the items on which they're bidding to be available at the end of the auction. You will disappoint a lot of your customers if you continually list and then revoke items from auction. It can be very frustrating to buyers. Consider any item you've listed on eBay to be committed to selling through eBay, and therefore unavailable through other sales channels as soon as the auction has a bidder.

sIngle iNventory

If you run a smaller business, with only a few employees, it may be easier for you to use only one inventory for all your sales channels—including eBay. This method requires close communication among employees and your smaller size lends itself to fast, constant, communication. Holding just one inventory also requires careful management of item availability, and integration of eBay into your existing inventory and accounting programs.

Using this method, you will not need an external eBay accounting program. Instead, just insert eBay sales into your existing sales program, noting the item's final sale price and marking eBay as the sales channel. This will integrate eBay sales into all your usual methods for accounting and produce the reports with which you are familiar. At the month's end you will need to tally all the eBay fees, PayPal fees, and subscription charges and insert them into your books as the expenses associated with selling on eBay. You can find these fees on your monthly eBay invoice, or throughout the month in your seller's account page.

The largest advantage to this single-inventory method is that you will not need to invest in a separate eBay inventory. Carrying tens of thousands of dollars worth of an extra inventory that is not available for sale in your showroom can seriously tax your cash flow. By using your main inventory as your eBay inventory you will be able to list all the items in your showroom, stock room, and storage for sale on eBay. This will instantly give you a formidable eBay inventory that will produce better traffic for your eBay Store and listings—which is a huge advantage over your competition. (For more on generating eBay traffic see Chapter 10, Marketing Strategies.)

There are some pitfalls. First, listing the items in your showroom for sale on eBay creates a situation where an item can be double-sold. To minimize this risk you need efficient communication between your sales staff and your eBay manager. Items that sell through your eBay Store or a fixed-price listing should be removed from your showroom floor and placed in a separate "eBay Staging Area" where the item waits for payment and shipment. The item should then be marked as sold in your company's inventory or sales manager so that other sales staff will know it is no longer available. This creates an always-up-to-date inventory database where your sales staff can track availability of items.

Auction items can be trickier. Unlike fixed-price items, an item can be spoken-for but unsold for up to 10 days. Items at auction that have no bids or watchers can be safely left on the showroom floor, and available to other sales channels. If there is zero interest in the item on eBay, there is no harm in ending the auction early and sending the item home with a happy local customer who wishes to purchase it. However, once the item receives a bid, the item is now unavailable for your other sales channels. To keep your inventory database up-to-date, items should be entered into your inventory manager as sold as soon as the first bid comes in. Leave the selling price and buyer information blank for the remaining duration of the auction. Or, if your inventory manager does not allow blank fields, use some dummy text that indicates the sale will be finalized once the auction ends.

Once the auction ends, return to the sales record in your sales program and fill in the final price and the winning bidder's information. Proceed with shipping as you normally would.

If you have an item that is listed in your eBay Store or in a fixed-price listing, and it sells from your showroom, the item must be removed from eBay. Upon the sale the showroom sales staff will record the sale just as they always would, and therefore the item would come out of available inventory. But the eBay sales manager must somehow become aware of this new sale so that the item can be removed from eBay. Either the sales manager must check showroom sales receipts or records periodically throughout the day, or he or she must be notified at the time of the sale.

The key for the single-inventory method to be successful is keeping an up-to-date inventory database and clear communication across sales personnel in all sales channels.

tRumbull's sTumbles

Trumbull Mountain started their eBay operation with a separate eBay inventory. They chose this method to reduce the risk of disappointing customers if an item sold in two places at once. All the eBay inventory was kept separate from the store's showroom inventory so that shoppers in their showroom wouldn't take home saddles designated to sell on eBay.

Once their dead stock pile had sold off, they were left with few items that were easily accessible to sell on eBay. To stock their eBay inventory, they selected highly eBayable items from their main inventory and converted them to eBay stock. They also submitted some eBay-specific orders from their major suppliers.

As their eBay inventory grew, the process they had worked out became extensive and expensive. Tens of thousands of dollars of inventory that formerly had been available to their more established sales channels was now sitting in a back room waiting to see if there was any interest on eBay. This tied up a lot of their most reliably selling inventory.

Also, the investment in new eBay-specific inventory grew to be substantial. The business found that it needed to stock its eBay inventory with a non-trivial amount of items. This extra investment was a large financial burden for Trumbull Mountain to carry.

Even with inventory from Trumbull Mountain's main inventory and the new investment in eBay inventory, the number of items Trumbull Mountain was able to list paled in comparison to some of their eBay competition. This meant that when a buyer searched for a saddle, over 90% of the listings shown were from competitors, meaning there was only a 10% chance that their items would ever be seen through searches.

The process of moving inventory out of the showroom and into the eBay stock was laborious. The staff was required to create a sales slip in the comany sales software for everything that was moving to the eBay department so that it was no longer in the showroom's inventory. This created a logistical and accounting headache.

To solve these problems Trumbull Mountain decided that it was a small enough business that it could communicate effectively enough to prevent double sales. They combined their two inventories into one. This stopped the staff from needing to create fictional sales slips to move inventory back and forth, integrated eBay sales into their existing sales manager, and allowed their eBay manager to list all of the inventory in the company—effectively tripling their eBay presence.

Trumbull Mountain now operates only one inventory, which they find to be cheaper and less of a hassle. The only drawback is that they need to be diligent in keeping the inventory database up-to-date and communicating sales between departments.

mUltiple lOcations

If your business has multiple locations, you will need to spend some time devising an eBay inventory strategy that best accommodates your needs. If you are selling mostly new items on eBay, you may consider setting up an eBay department in one of your locations that deals with ordering and selling new eBay items. If you plan on selling existing stock from multiple locations, you will most likely need to consolidate that inventory into one location before it can be properly dealt with. Your final option is to set up an eBay department at each location wherein the staff is trained to manage eBay sales independently.

jUst-in-tIme Inventory

One of the huge benefits of eBay is the short turnover time with which you can sell products. If you are dealing mainly with auctions, the longest you should ever need to stock an item is 10 days—the length of the longest auctions. If you have done your research well enough, you should be listing items that are in high enough demand that they sell near 100% of the time. If this is the case, you will know that if you list six items, then six will sell. If that's so, you have no need to tie up valuable cash in inventory as you know exactly when you will need to send off those six items. As long as the items arrive before they are due to ship, you will be in the clear, and your cash reserves will be readily available.

Obviously this practice of managing a just-in-time-inventory requires a lot of practice, research, and finesse. You will need to know exactly how likely it is that an item will sell, exactly the amount of time needed to receive the item, and the average price you will receive for the item. Being just-in-time does you no good if you are shipping off unprofitable items.

For longer-term store listings that last for 30 days at a time, and no pressing time limit, the just-in-time method is less useful. If your business aims to sell more items through your eBay Store, where prices are fixed and profits are guaranteed, then running a just-in-time-inventory may be a luxury you can't logistically pull off. As your items can sell at any moment, you will have a harder time predicting the exact moment you will need items in inventory.

Both methods have their virtues. Just-in-time inventory will free up your cash for high-turnover, high-volume, auction-based businesses. A conventional inventory with a high investment in stock is necessary for fixed-price-based operations, but profits are guaranteed.

dRop sHipping

Some eBay businesses find drop-shipping to be a useful alternative to carrying large amounts of inventory. Drop-shipping is a practice where retailers don't purchase items from the source until they sell through the retailer. Upon sale, the item is shipped directly from the item's source to the purchasing customer. This hop over the retailer means that items don't need to sit in the retailer's warehouse or shelves. No investment is made in carrying inventory.

Many manufacturers, distributors, and other product sources offer a drop-shipping program. At first this solution may sound like the perfect situation: your business buys no inventory, manages no inventory, and does zero shipping. However, this relationship can be fraught with problems. Often the communication between retailer and product source is too slow and items that were once available are no longer. Also, as retailers are no longer in charge of shipping, they have little recourse if a customer complains about slow or nonexistent shipping. By removing your company from this vital aspect of customer care you are placing your reputation in the hands of an outside company with possibly too little interest in your reputation.

If you are considering drop-shipping, be sure to do so only with a supplier with which you've worked for many years. And, then only do so for their most popular items—as they're likely to have plenty in stock at all times.

eChapter five

Photography

for all its virtues, eBay is inherently flawed in one major respect: the "touch-and-feel" factor. People shopping at everyday retail stores like Best Buy, or Target, or an Apple store, are encouraged to pick up and manhandle the items in the store. This provides buyers with a level of familiarity with items that eBay can never offer. The experiences of weight, texture, and durability are difficult to translate to the online shopper, but this is exactly your task as item photographer. Your photography should recreate, as closely as possible, the in-store shopping experience.

Creating successful photos will require careful consideration at every step of the process. It can be quite time-consuming to define and refine the process to a point where it is adequately streamlined for efficient everyday use. Luckily though, your equipment need not be the top-of-the-line, and the materials necessary for a proper studio setup can be found inexpensively.

The importance of creating good photos of your items cannot be understated. Items without photos sell pathetically on eBay, if at all. Items with poor photography sell only marginally better. This chapter will define what "good" means when it comes to eBay photography. The tools and techniques in this chapter will help you to create photos of your items that stand out from the photos of your competitors,

hElpful hInt

Your item photography provides a great opportunity for you to separate your business from your competition. With just some simple changes to the basic technique and setup, you can produce photos that are vastly better than 99% of the photos currently on eBay.

reflect the professionalism of your business, and convert your listings to sales.

tHe cAmera

The most vital part of this photography process is, of course, the camera. Contrary to what you might be fearing, you do not need an expensive camera to produce professional-quality photography. The high quality of cameras on the market these days pretty much ensures that any new camera would be more than adequate for your purposes, but for excellent photos, there are some features you will need.

First off, you will need a digital camera. The laborious process necessary to use a film camera for this task makes digital the clear winner. Digital cameras have come down in price in recent years and many of your local stores—Staples, OfficeMax, Best Buy, Circuit City—are sure to have an adequate selection.

When shopping for digital cameras you will first notice that each camera has a "megapixel" rating. This rating does not speak to the camera's quality, only the size of the images it is able to produce. Do not get sucked into the marketer's pitch that more megapixels equals more quality. That simply isn't true.

A megapixel can be defined as one million (mega) picture elements (pixel). The higher the number of megapixels a camera can produce, the higher the resolutions of the photos it produces will be. This rating really only applies to professional photographers who plan on printing their work, since they need to know that the photos they are capturing will be of high enough resolution upon printing to not look fuzzy. You do not need high resolution photos as your photos will be displayed on a computer monitor with far lower resolution requirements, usually only 72 dpi (dots per inch). Figure 5-1 displays the megapixel ratings of the most common computer monitor resolutions. As you can see in Figure 5-1, the most common screen resolution of 1024 x 768 can only display 0.8 megapixel images at full size with a pixel ratio of 1:1.

In summary, a 3-megapixel camera will suffice, and a 6-megapixel camera will be more than adequate. The latter can be found for around $300.

Monitor Type	Megapixel Rating	Resolution
VGA	0.3 Megapixels	640×480
SVGA	0.5 Megapixels	800×600
XVGA	0.8 Megapixels	1024×768
SXGA	1.3 Megapixels	1280×1024
UXGA	1.9 Megapixels	1600×1200
QXGA	3.1 Megapixels	2048×1536
QSXGA	5.2 Megapixels	2560×2048

Figure 5-1.

If you have more than $300 to budget for a camera, explore digital SLR (single-lens reflex) cameras. SLR cameras are unlike the most common type of digital camera with the small LCD screen on the back. Instead, they use a lens and shutter system more like traditional cameras. Instead of looking at an LCD screen the photographer looks through a more traditional viewfinder, which looks out through the camera's actual lens. This provides the photographer the advantage of seeing the image exactly as it will be captured, whereas LCD screens can offset the image in one direction or another and have their own interpretations of color and shadow.

hElpful hInt

SLR cameras also have the advantage of allowing for interchangeable lenses—normal, macro, wide, telephoto, and so on—for more flexibility.

Independent of the camera style you select, your final choice should have the following options.

Macro: The macro option (or lens) uses an very short focal distance. This allows the camera to take extremely detailed close-up shots of items without losing focus. You will find that this ability is necessary for photographing your item's details, smallest parts, or flaws without blurring.

Zoom: Most any camera you purchase these days will have some sort of zoom function. You will find this the feature you will use most often, as zooming in or out is much easier than moving the tripod back and forth.

There are two types of zoom that you should be aware of: optical zoom and digital zoom. Cameras using optical zoom are capable of physically moving their lenses to adjust the size of the image in the viewfinder. This is how traditional cameras performed the zoom function. Digital zoom, however, is performed entirely by the camera's internal software—digitally increasing the size of the image in the camera's viewfinder.

Generally speaking, you won't notice much difference between the two zoom methods unless you need to do significant zooming in on your products. If you find that to be the case however, select a camera with a strong optical zoom. When a camera uses optical zoom to zoom in on an item, the amount of light information entering the camera does not change—only the way the light enters the camera changes. Therefore the camera is able to create a final image file of the new, zoomed image with just as much information as would have been created had the photographer not zoomed in. However, zooming with a digital zoom camera is performed by increasing the size of each pixel in the non-zoomed image and cutting off the edges of the larger photo to fit the viewfinder. The amount of pixel information in the photo is decreased, and therefore the image's maximum resolution is decreased. This creates potential for fuzzy photos.

USB: Every digital camera has a method for connecting to a computer. Some use media cards, some use cables, some use docking stations, and some now even connect wirelessly. The fastest and most universal method for connecting a digital camera to your computer is through a technology called USB 2.0. USB stands for Universal Serial Bus. The new 2.0 version of USB can transmit 480 megabytes of data every second from your camera to your computer. What this means is that it is capable of moving all the data from a 512 MB media card to your computer in just over a second, or a 1 GB card in just over two.

Most computers built within the last two years come with a USB 2.0 port either on the front of the computer, the back, or on the system's keyboard (mostly available on Macs). If your computer is older than two years, don't fret—USB 2.0 is "backwards-compatible" and will work in any USB port, although only at 12 MB per second.

Using a camera with a USB 2.0 port, you will be able to take all the photos you need, sit down at your desk, plug in the camera's USB cable, and have all your photos on your computer in a few seconds. This is much easier than using a media card reader, which requires you to swap media cards from your camera to your computer and back. USB is just plug-and-go, and it works with nearly every computer.

Flash Control: It is necessary that you are able to turn off your camera's flash function. In this type of photography a flash will often create a ghastly glare across the front of your items, and a dark shadow behind them. Permanent, softer light is preferable to the harshness of flash bulbs.

LCD Review: Any digital camera with an LCD screen will allow you to review the images you've just captured. If you opt for an SLR digital camera, be sure that it also has an LCD for reviewing images (even though you won't be using the LCD as the viewfinder). Instant review of your images makes your job much easier as you won't need to move photos to you computer to see if they turned out satisfactorily. You can edit on the fly.

Media Cards: All digital cameras allow for internal storage of images. The methods they use to store your images, however, will vary. Most cameras use standardized media cards of varying sizes, and a few use internal, permanent hard drives. Select a camera that uses a standard media card format. They allow you to upgrade the camera's internal storage capacity if you find yourself needing to empty the camera too often. Also, cameras that use this type of storage have fewer internal moving parts than their hard drive counterparts and are therefore less susceptible to damage from bumping or knocking. Plus, if a media card goes south, it is easily replaced. If your camera's hard drive dies, you'd need a new camera.

hElpful hInt

Trumbull Mountain uses a Kodak EasyShare Z740 5 megapixel camera to photograph their saddles and bridles and girths and such. The 5 megapixels gives them the sharpness they need to capture the texture of the saddle leather, and the macro function allows them to capture details like stitching, labels, and branding. They have also found it to be quite easy to use with both their Macintosh and Windows computers.

yOur pHoto sTudio

The layout and permanence of your photo "studio" will depend on the size of your items and inventory. If you sell small items like MP3 players or cell phones, your setup may only need to be as large as one end of your shipping table. However, if you sell larger items like pool tables or car seats, your studio will need to be laid out in a way that accommodates the particular shape and size of your items.

Sellers of new items may need to take photos only occasionally. For example, if you sell brand-new computer RAM modules, you will not need to photograph every individual RAM module you sell. Because every module will look exactly like the one sold previously, one set of photographs for each type of RAM module that you sell will work for every auction or listing you post. Selling brand-new, identical items can save you heaps of time dealing with photos, and means that the photo setup itself need only be temporary.

Most sellers do not have this luxury. eBay buyers are sticklers for details. They want to know the condition of the items they're purchasing right down to the last scratch and scuff. Any sellers of used items will need to photograph each item they list in painstaking detail. Each mark should be recorded in a photo and noted in the description. This gives buyers the opportunity to accurately judge how much they want to pay for the item. It also protects sellers from negative feedback later when a buyer receives an item whose condition has been generously stated.

Sellers of unique, used, or any other type of non-identical, non-assembly line items will need a permanent photo setup, the size and setup of which will be determined by the type of items you're selling.

To minimize the amount of time you spend juggling your inventory, consider where your photography studio should fall along your inventory's item flow. If possible, find a space between where you receive your items and where they are ultimately stored while on sale. In this manner, your items can proceed from receiving, to photography, to inventory, to shipping in one fluid process—minimizing the time you spend sorting out which inventory should be at the different stages.

Once you've chosen a suitable location, it is time to begin putting the pieces together. If selling larger items that require floor space, your setup should back up to a permanent wall, which will function as your backdrop. On this wall you should hang a white backdrop material. Smaller items can be placed on a tabletop in front of a white backdrop—paper, cardboard, or the like.

> **hElpful hInt**
>
> Trumbull Mountain chose sheets of white felt to hang behind their saddles. The felt reflects light well without any glare or wrinkles. It can be found inexpensively at any local department store.

Lighting your items can be difficult. There are a number of factors to consider. First, you will need plenty of light shining down on your items. Photos taken in dimly lit rooms will produce muddy, dark, unexciting photos. Sunlight is the best, as it will best translate the item's actual color to the camera lens. But, even if you have a gigantic, south-facing picture window to photograph underneath, sunlight can create problematic shadows and glare.

The best thing to do when setting up your studio is to plan for multiple light sources, from multiple angles. You should place your item in a central position, and plan to hang or clip lights to either side, and directly in front of your item. The ability to move and adjust lighting is critical, so try to find lamps that are easy to move. By placing lamps to either side of the item you are achieving two goals: you are canceling out unwanted shadows, and you are providing large amounts of light with the lowest chance for glare. You will need to test many lighting configurations before you find one that produces the least glare, and even then you might need to use diffusing techniques, depending on the item you're photographing.

> ## mOney mAnagement
>
> Any hardware store will carry "clamp lamps" that are often used on construction sites. These metal lamps are shaped in a way that allows you to direct light effectively. The strong clamp lets you clip the lamp to almost any surface. The one drawback is that these lights get hot fast when using incandescent bulbs. Use a compact fluorescent bulb to keep the lamps cool and to save on electricity.

In addition to a camera, a backdrop, and lighting there are a few other items you'll need to fully equip your studio. Here's a quick list.

Tripod. You will need a tripod for a number of reasons. The most obvious is that it holds the camera steady and prevents blurring. But also important is that a tripod will free you up to make adjustments to your lighting, your item's angle, and your backdrop as needed. By keeping the camera fixed in one location you can design your shots more accurately.

Drawing Paper. When photographing glossy items or items sealed in plastic, the light that falls on your items will be too harsh. The items will have glare bouncing off them in every direction and dramatic shadows that ruin the shot. Clipping translucent drawing paper up in front of your light sources will diffuse the light and cast a softer glow down upon your items, neutralizing the glare and shadows.

Clothespins. Clothespins are quite handy to have around your studio. Not only can they clip drawing paper over lights, as mentioned above, but they can help you hold your backdrop in place, hold pieces of the item at certain angles, and hold the cords from your lights up out of the photos. There's no end to how handy these can be.

Clamps. In addition to clothespins, you will want to get a few stronger clamps. Trumbull Mountain finds that sturdy clamps are useful to hold the heavy saddle flaps open for their saddle detail shots, to hang heavy leather items in front of the photo backdrop, and a few other uses that clothespins couldn't handle.

Stepladder. Sometimes you will need to photograph from an angle that you wouldn't be able to reach without a stepladder. Photographing the tops of items while they are tilted to their side can be awkward and does not produce the desired effect. To get up above your items, or to adjust your backdrop, or to adjust your lighting, a simple stepladder will do the trick. Find one that folds up easily for convenient storage while not in use.

Black Backdrop. While a white backdrop is ideal for most photo applications, there may come a time when you are photographing a white object (such as an iPod) when a black backdrop would be more suitable. In these cases you can clip up a black bed sheet or shower curtain over your existing white backdrop.

tHe iMage

One casual round of browsing of photography on eBay—in any category—will reveal thousands of dark, confusing, misleading photographs of items. In the interest of speed or laziness many sellers have opted to put in the least amount of effort possible when creating their photographs. For many casual sellers, it simply isn't worth their time to spend half an hour photographing the old copy of SimCity that they're selling for $0.99. So they snap an image of the game's box on their cluttered desk with their low-resolution webcam. Other sellers invest substantial time and snap 30 photographs per item, but they end up with 30 poor images due to their poor technique.

By thinking through the goal of each image before you snap the picture you can improve the quality of your photography and increase the professionalism of your listing. The most basic goal of each image you create is to convey information. Whether it be the size or shape or color or design of the item, the photo is the best way to inform your buyers about the specific nature of the item up for sale.

The first image you should consider is the item's primary image. This will be the image that will load first on the item's description and most likely as the gallery photo displayed in eBay's search results. This image will serve as your "overall" image. The goal of this image is not to single out specific qualities of the item, but to give your buyers a clear idea of the item as a whole. This photo should stress accurate color, size, shape, and angles.

You can achieve the most accurate color representation in your photos by using natural sunlight or special photography bulbs that produce a 5000 K color temperature daylight balanced light. These special bulbs can be found on eBay or at most any photography shop. They are inexpensive ($30 to $60) and come in a variety of shapes, sizes, and brightnesses. You can find both incandescent and fluorescent bulbs that are made to fit standard sockets.

For items where size can be a factor in your buyer's purchasing decision, you will need to find a way to give an indication of the item's size. Listing the item's dimensions in the description will help, but the buyer needs a visual indication as well. For example, the size of MP3 players can vary drastically. A buyer may be looking for the smallest MP3 possible, but if your photo gives no point of reference for the item's size, the buyer may end up with a MP3 player the size of a football, or, more likely, they'll move on to buy one they can be sure is small enough. A popular trick is to place a quarter in the photo alongside the item as a size reference.

Obviously, placing a quarter on the ground next to a motorcycle will do nobody—except the next passerby—any good. For larger items, use a more appropriately sized, but equally familiar, object. Using a human subject is sometimes helpful. For instance, placing a person on the motorcycle gives a fairly good indication of the bike's size. However, as people come in all shapes and sizes, it could be difficult for the buyer to guess a person's size relative to their own. Children can sometimes come in handy, as we can better judge a child's size by his or her approximate age.

In the main image of your item you should present the item in the most flattering angle. (The flaws will be covered well enough in the detail shots.) Placing a DVD case flat down on the table is not presenting it from its best angle. Prop up flat items to better reflect the light and to showcase their colors. This gives the flat items an "active" look that is better at exciting the buyer's emotional connection to the item.

If your items simply don't have an exciting angle or position—a deck of cards, for instance—then you can try placing the item into a mock setting. By placing the deck of cards on some green felt and tossing some poker chips around it, you will provide the buyer with an exciting context through with to look at the item. Now, instead of selling a pack of cards on an empty table, you're selling your deck of cards that has the capability for action, adventure, and international intrigue.

In every photo you take, whether it is for the main description photo, the gallery photo, or any of the detail shots, you will need to single out your item as the photo's main subject. Clutter in the background of an image will distract your buyers and could confuse them as to what's actually being sold. If you've dedicated a space to your photo studio and hung a backdrop, then clutter shouldn't be a problem for you. If you haven't been able to dedicate a space for photography yet, then be sure to frame your photos in such a way that your item is clearly at the center of the photo, if not the only thing in it.

You can use your camera's focus field to focus in on your item, but blur out the busy background. Also, you can elevate the angle of the photo to capture the item from above, with nothing but table top behind it. In both cases, make sure that the item is lit well from all angles. Without dedicated light sources, quick photos will look unprofessional.

sTrategy sNippet

Creating an infinite horizon behind your image is a great way to create beautiful photos of smaller items. This can be done by first placing a thin sheet of white paperboard flat on a table. Place your item on the closest half of the white paperboard and then pull the farther half up so that it curves gently toward the sky. Place any convenient object behind the paperboard to prop it up behind the item. Light this setup well and you will have a quick and cheap way to create great photos with no background, creases, or clutter to disrupt the photo.

In all likelihood, there are sellers on eBay selling items that are exactly like yours. This can lead to problems when those sellers take the time-saving shortcut of taking the photos you've spent hours creating and using them in their own auctions and listings. This is against eBay policy and if you can prove it, you should report these offending sellers to eBay. But, unfortunately, eBay cannot prevent the practice. The very nature of the Internet means that your photos will be loaded on thousands of other people's computers. Saving one for later can be done by anybody browsing eBay.

So to protect yourself and the effort you put into your photographs, you should place a watermark on each image you create. A watermark is a way of indiscreetly stamping your company's logo onto your images. They are most effective in preventing theft when spread across the center of the image with a 90-95% translucency that allows buyers to see the item underneath, but prevents other sellers from being able to edit the watermark out of the image. Most eBay sellers prefer to place a watermark in the corner of an image where it isn't obstructing the view of the image in any way. This is better than nothing, but as offending sellers can just snip off that corner of the image, it won't do much good against ambitious photo-thieves.

Most popular photo editing programs can provide you with watermarks, or, if not, plug-ins or utility applications can provide you with watermarks.

pHoto mAnagement sOftware

Dealing with photos can be the most time-consuming aspect of selling on eBay. After setting up the photo station, configuring the lights, taking the photos, and transferring them to your computer you've already spent hours of your work day on the process. A quality photo management system goes a long way toward making the post–photoshoot process less painful.

Luckily you won't need any software that is too elaborate or expensive. The tasks of naming and grouping and editing photos can achieved relatively simply. The following programs are popular among established eBay sellers.

Photoshop

The industry standard of photo manipulation software is Adobe's Photoshop. This program is one of the oldest and most respected photo editing applications available. It can be used by amateurs and professionals alike. It runs on the expensive side at $610 for the latest version

(Photoshop CS2), and does not perform any photo collection management functions. It is strictly for photo editing, but if you want top-of-the-line photo editing capabilities, this is where you'll find it. You might also consider Adobe Photoshop Elements, which has most of the functions you'll need and costs much less. Visit **www.adobe.com** for more information.

The GIMP

Despite its curious name, GIMP is a well-respected, professional-quality photo editing program that some would argue is on a par with Photoshop. GIMP is an acronym for GNU Image Manipulation Program. (GNU is another acronym and is the name of the open-source license under which the program is published.) The major difference between Photoshop and GIMP is that the latter is, and will remain, completely free. Find out more at **www.gimp.org**.

Google's Picasa

Unlike Photoshop and GIMP, Picasa, from Google, is designed to be a photo organization and management program. It's designed to help users transfer photos off any modern digital camera and into the program's own organization system. Users can group, rename, and send photos to a web server, e-mail, or blog. It also allows users to make basic edits to photos, such as cropping and adjusting brightness and color balance. For eBay photo management purposes Picasa covers the basics very well. It is a free program and is available at **www.picasa.com**.

Apple's iPhoto

iPhoto is the photo organization and optimization tool that Picasa tries to emulate. iPhoto is part of the iLife suite of programs that comes loaded on any Apple computer. It does a great job in transferring your photos off any modern digital camera and organizing your eBay photos into custom albums (saddles, apparel, fittings, etc.) and also, automatically, by date and time. Finding photos you've taken years ago for any purpose is quite easy. iPhoto provides basic editing tools such as cropping, automatic photo enhancement, red-eye reduction, and color adjustments. iPhoto is only available for Macs, but the good news is that if you have a somewhat modern Mac now (OS X and higher), you have iPhoto. Learn more about the programs capabilities at **www.apple.com/iphoto**.

sTorage

If you've ever made the mistake of attempting to e-mail a photograph that came directly from your camera, then you're already aware: the files are enormous. They can range in size from 1 to 10 megabytes per file, depending on your camera and its settings. The amount of storage space on your computer will dwindle fast once you start unloading your camera onto it. But you have no alternative. So how do you deal with it?

There are many methods of storing photos that won't bog down your computer. The first option is to archive all your old photos to recordable CDs. The process of selecting old images to archive, burning them to a disc, and then storing that disc away in some sort of organized, retrievable manner can be painfully slow. CDs have a shelf-life of no more than seven years, and therefore this can only be a temporary solution.

> ### hElpful hInt
>
> Trumbull Mountain invested in a photo-only computer with an internal 300 GB hard drive. They also boosted the RAM to 2 GB to speed up photo editing. This allows them fast access to all their photos without needing to worry about running out of space. They have now room for approximately 300,000 photos.

Another option is to buy an external, high-capacity hard drive with 300 to 500 GB of storage space. An external drive will connect to your computer very easily via a USB or FireWire cable, and will allow for fast transfer and more permanent, and easier accessed, storage for your photos. Plus, because the hard drive is contained in its own unit separate from the computer, you will have the option to move the images from one file to the next.

No matter which file storage system you choose, you will need to use a file-naming system that associates the individual image files with their respective items. Trumbull Mountain uses a variation of each item's internal inventory code to name each image file. This works well for them as they can tell exactly what any image file contains without spending the time to open the image. Then they use iPhoto keep the photos organized by item category and year, month, and day. iPhoto does all of this for them so they can concentrate on other things.

hElpful hInt

Be sure to back up your photo files. You put a lot of work into creating these professional photos, and you need to protect them. They represent thousands of dollars of employee time. Use specific backup software to back up your photo archive regularly, and automatically. Apple provides their users with the easy-to-use and simply titled program, Backup. Windows users can find a range of options across the Internet.

gEtting yOur pHotos to eBay

There are several ways to get your photos onto your auction and listing pages. You can use eBay's own photo hosting, which is easy to do simply by uploading your photos during the listing process, but the privilege will cost you $0.15 for every photo after the first. When listing 10 photos per item and hundreds (or thousands) of listings per month, this expense is not feasible.

There are less expensive photo hosting services available (see Appendix C) and many of them offer eBay-specific tools to help sellers. For a low monthly fee (from free to $15/month) you are given a limited amount of space on the hosting service's servers. Then, when eBay asks you to provide photos for your item, instead of uploading photos to eBay's expensive service, you simply provide the URLs for your images for free. It costs eBay no more money to display as many photos as you would like to post, but it costs them quite a bit in server maintenance to store your photos on their servers.

While photo hosting services can save you a lot of money in the long run, they may be an expense you don't need to pay. As an established business you likely already have a web site up and running. The hosting service that you pay to keep your web site online is already providing the same service to you as any of the specific eBay photo hosting companies. Instead of paying another monthly fee, you need only to create a special directory on your web site's server and upload all your photos there. When eBay asks you for your auction photos, you can simply provide the URL to the appropriate image in that new directory on your web site. For example: www.mycompany.com/ ebay/photos/sample_image.jpg.

This method will save you money by taking full advantage of the services for which you're already paying. A word of caution though: your web site's web host account will have a storage capacity limit, which you may quickly reach if you upload too many photos. Reaching your storage capacity will limit the growth of your existing web site. You can either delete all the photos from your web host that are not currently at auction (some eBay sellers clean out the photo directory every week and then upload a new batch when they start their weekly auctions), or you can contact your web host and ask for a storage limit increase.

eBay's Selling Options

Bay offers several ways for you to sell your items. These various selling formats can be confusing, as they each contain a multitude of options, time frames, and requirements. New sellers are often baffled by the intricacies of Buy It Now prices, reserve prices, and starting prices. And everybody gets understandably tripped up by the difference between "Fixed Price" listings and "fixed price" listings. Yes, there is a difference, and I'll explain it in this chapter.

The three main selling formats are auctions, Fixed Price listings, and store listings. Auctions are the most popular, and most well-known, of the selling formats. Every seller, regardless of experience or feedback rating, can create an auction listing. They are eBay's foundation and strongest draw.

Sellers who meet a certain set of eBay's requirements have access to the Fixed Price listing format. These Fixed Price listings are like auctions in that they are formatted similarly, share many of the same listing options, and are inserted alongside auctions in eBay's main search results. However, no bidding takes place in Fixed Priced listings. The price you set doesn't change.

Sellers who have subscribed to the eBay Store program are able to sell items through the store format. Like the Fixed Price listings, the prices of store items do not change. Store listings do not appear in eBay's main search results and can last up to 30 days at a time.

This chapter will provide you with an overview of the different selling formats, and the elements of each, so that when the time comes for you to begin formulating your advanced selling strategies, you can put the particular advantages of each format to good use.

aUctions

Auctions used to comprise the whole of eBay's offerings. They now serve as the site's foundation and as a main draw for buyers. There are high-end computer systems, diamond-studded watches, cars, and even houses with starting prices of only one dollar. The allure is obvious. Every day shoppers from all over the world pick through eBay's millions of auctions hunting for the one, unknown, unseen, bargain of the century. These millions of auction shoppers create what I refer to as the "auction stream." This auction stream is the constant river of buyer traffic that courses through eBay's auction listings every day. Your goal is to divert some of that flow into your own auctions, fixed-price listings, and eBay Store.

In 2006 eBay boasted 1 billion page views per day, with roughly 26 billion database searches per day. Searches performed through eBay's main search box, which is placed on nearly every eBay page, search only one thing: auction titles. It is possible, through the advanced search function, to search every corner of eBay, but the overwhelming majority of searches performed on eBay only return results found in auction titles. This makes two things perfectly clear: your auction titles must be effective; and your eBay Store items are—for all intents and purposes—invisible to searching.

There are as many strategies concerning the use of auctions as there are auctions themselves. An auction listing has many strategic tools at your disposal: starting price, Buy It Now price, reserve price, length of auction, bold, border, gallery photo, featured listing, and more. The right combination of all of these promotional elements is debated in every corner of the Internet. Finding what works best for you will require a combination of research, testing, and good-ole' wild guessing.

---

hElpful hInt

The eBay research tools from Andale provide members with a "How to Sell" feature, which analyzes all the data from all the sales for a given keyword and produces a report detailing the most successful combination of elements for the given item. It will tell you what combination of starting time, starting price, and listing upgrades have produced the highest final sale price in the recent past.

---

fIxed pRice lIstings

A Fixed Price listing is similar to an auction. It is formatted exactly the same. It offers the same starting time and duration options. It even appears alongside auctions in eBay's main search results. The only difference is that instead of setting a starting price, you simply set the item's fixed price. There is no bidding.

eBay, in one of its dimwitted moments, gave this option the short-sighted name of Fixed Price Listing, which, when it was introduced, stood in stark contrast to the only other available selling format at the time: auctions. But, after the introduction of the eBay Stores program with their fixed-price, store-format listings, the once black and white definition of Fixed Price Listings had shades of gray. eBay further muddied the water when they introduced Buy It Now (BIN) prices. These BIN prices are fixed prices sellers can offer on auctions. "Fixed Price Listing," as eBay uses it, refers solely to listings that are inserted into the main auction stream but do not allow bidding. The term "fixed price listing" when used by the eBay user community or by eBay management tools can refer to either eBay's "Fixed Price Listing" format, or to the eBay Store listing format, or to BIN prices, since all of them use fixed prices.

sTore lIstings

The items you stock into your eBay Store will have a duration of 30 days and can be set to relist automatically upon the expiration of that duration. Effectively, these are permanent listings (until sold) that you pay for every 30 days.

Items in your eBay Store do not show up in eBay's main search results, and therefore it takes some extra promotion to lure shoppers into your store. I'll discuss store marketing techniques more in Chapter 10, Marketing Strategies.

Holding a store inventory is a great way to upsell more items. Listings are cheap at either $0.05 or $0.10 for 30 days, and they can provide you with great opportunity for profits. Linking to store items from your auction pages is a great way to sell extra items associated with your main product. Trumbull Mountain promotes their bridles, saddle pads, bits, and such on each of their saddle auction pages. This gives buyers an opportunity to buy all the "goes-with-its" from you for a low combined shipping cost.

lIsting tItle

The title of your auction or fixed-price listing is the most important real estate you have on eBay. This title must include all the most likely search terms that buyers might use to find the item, must describe the item in somewhat human-readable form, and must grab the attention of buyers who are quickly scanning the search results page. Mashing these three tasks together would be difficult to do if you had 1,000 words to do it in, but eBay makes it nearly impossible by allowing you only 55 characters.

Any letter, number, punctuation mark, space, or symbol is counted toward your 55-character limit. If you find that there is no possible way to accomplish all that you need to within 55 characters, you do have the option to spill over into the subtitle field, but that will cost you $0.50 and the keywords entered here are not searchable in any way.

Punctuation will generally not help you, and in some instances, it will hurt you. Commas, dashes, apostrophes, and such only take up valuable space that you should be filling up with searchable keywords. The only place that punctuation is a good idea is if you think that a buyer would use that punctuation mark in their search, as they might when searching for model numbers (Mac mini M9687LL/A) or item specifications (1.66 GHz Mac mini).

Good titles combine keywords and item specifics in a legible format without too much (or any) wasted space. The following two examples were taken from actual eBay listings. They are selling an identical item.

*NIB APPLE IPOD NANO ... EARPHONES, USB CABLE..L@@K

NEW Apple iPod Nano 4GB Color Silver 2nd Gen MA426LL/A

Both titles are within the 55-character limit. However, the first example provides few searchable keywords. The only three likely keywords (APPLE, IPOD, and NANO) will do nothing to help buyers find this specific iPod. Much of the available space is wasted on odd punctuation and eye-catching gimmicks that do not work. No model number is given, which puts the seller at a huge disadvantage since model numbers are one of the most popular search methods buyers use to find an item.

The second example is far better. The seller has wasted no space on unnecessary punctuation, using it only where it is required in the item's model number. The title provides clear information about the item's capabilities and condition. It provides at least six likely search terms and wastes no space on eye-grabbing gimmicks.

If you're unsure which keywords to use in your titles, it can be helpful to do a search for similar items on eBay. What keywords are other sellers using? What keywords are the most successful sellers using?

In each auction title you create, you should include:

- brand name
- model number
- item specifics (color, size, capacity, speed, model year, etc.)
- condition (new, used, mint, etc.)

Blue Star Computers has an entire warehouse of computer components. Even though each component was taken out of a specific model computer, many of them would work perfectly well inside several similar model computers from the same manufacturer. For example, an LCD screen that was salvaged from a Dell Inspirion 1100 notebook computer would be a suitable replacement screen not only for the Inspirion 1100 model, but also for the Inspirion 2600, and 2650. By including the additional model numbers in the screen's auction title, Blue Star is able to pull in significantly more traffic from owners of all three of the various models, not just the original one. Many of their auction titles now include a number of suitable computer model numbers, along with the original part number. For example:

DELL LCD PANEL 14.1 XGA INSPIRON 1100 2600 2650 2N066

If you are creating an auction without a reserve price, and you have an extra three spaces in your title, tag " NR" at the end of your auction to signify that your auction has "No Reserve." Auctions without reserves draw in more bidders, and therefore, often higher final sale prices. See Appendix D for a more complete list of standard eBay listing title abbreviations that you can safely use in your titles to save space.

All listings have titles, whether they are auctions, Fixed Price listings, or items in your store. Every listing title is subject to the same restrictions, and should follow the same guidelines.

listing uPgrades

Every item you list will have available listing upgrades. These upgrades change the appearance of your listing in eBay's main search results. The upgrades you select, and the manner in which you present your item listing to eBay buyers, will determine your listing fee. For example, a basic seven-day listing with a one-dollar starting price and no upgrades will cost you only a $0.20 listing fee. (The total fees for this sale will include the listing fee, plus the final value fees. See Appendix B for the eBay fee structure.) You can elect to upgrade that listing, in the hopes that it becomes more visible among the other listings on the results page by bolding your title for $1.00, or adding a gallery photo for $0.35, or border for $3.00, or highlighting for $5.00. Adding these, or any of the 18 available upgrades, may bring your listing more traffic, and therefore a higher sale price. However, they may also flop. If no demand for the item you're auctioning exists on eBay, no amount of upgrades will make your item more popular, and you're just wasting money.

I suggest you always select to add at least a gallery photo and bold. Selecting to use a gallery photo will place an image of your item into eBay's search results page and has been shown to increase the final sale price of items by 11%. Bolding your listing title in the search results page increases your listing's visibility and has been shown to increase final sale price by an average of 25%. For higher-priced, or rare items, I suggest you use eBay's Featured Plus package for $19.95. The Featured Plus package will display your item in the category's "Featured Items" box and will display your item at the top of all the appropriate search pages, as well as among the usual listings. Featured Plus has been shown to increase sales rates by 28%. That's quite a boost, but you must consider the package's high price when the item's profit margins may be slim.

sTarting tImes and dUration

Every listing you submit to eBay will have a duration and a starting time. For store items, these two factors are irrelevant as these listings are usually relisted right away and are therefore always available. For auction items and Fixed Price listings, however, these two factors can play a large role in the overall success of your sale.

Auctions can run for 1, 3, 5, 7, or 10 days. Your base listing fee allows you to choose from any duration under, and including, 7 days. Ten-day auctions cost an extra $0.40. The duration of your auction is accurate to the second. So, if you submit a 7-day auction at 7 pm on Monday night, the auction will end 604,800 seconds later at 7 pm the following Monday night. This is significant.

eBay's search results can be sorted in a variety of ways, but the two most popular methods are to sort listings by "newly listed" and by "ending soonest," while the site's default method is "ending soonest." Therefore, your listing is most visible at two points in its duration: when it is first listed, and in the listing's closing minutes. Studies have shown that aligning your auction's ending time with a time of the week that eBay experiences heavy traffic increases your sales rates and final sale prices. The more shoppers there are on the site, the more chance your item has of reaching the right set of eyes.

All the PowerSellers we've spoken with indicate that Sunday evening is generally the best time to end an auction. Monday comes in a distant second. Ideally you will grow to a point where you will have auctions ending at all times of day, all week long, but before you reach that point, it is best to plan for your items to be most visible when eBay provides the largest audience.

sTrategy sNippet

Peak eBay Traffic Times

Eighty percent of eBay shoppers find items through the site's search function. The default method of displaying search results places the items that have the fewest minutes remaining at the top, and then in ascending order down the page. This means that your item is most visible at the end of its run. By aligning the end of your auction with eBay's peak traffic times you can ensure that your auction is receiving its maximum potential traffic.

Below is a list of eBay's highest traffic times to help you coordinate ending times.

Days of the week, from busiest to slowest:
Sunday
Monday
Thursday
Saturday
Tuesday
Wednesday
Friday

Times of day, from busiest to slowest: (eBay Time: PST)
  6 pm–9 pm
  9 pm–12 am
  3 pm–6 pm
  12 pm–3 pm
  9 am–12 pm
  6 am–9 am
  12 am–3 am
  3 am–6 am

Ending your auctions on Sunday evening between 6 pm and 9 pm is generally regarded as the best time to do so. Beware, though, of holidays and Super Bowl Sunday. Pop your head up out of the world of eBay every so often to find out if there are mitigating circumstances that would change eBay's traffic patterns.

During the times that your listings receive the most traffic, you will receive the most questions about your items. If you line up all your auctions to end on one night you could very well end up with an inbox full of questions from potential buyers in a matter of hours. If you choose Sunday night to end your auctions, you will most likely be left with an inbox packed with excited shoppers, but with nobody in the office to serve them. This can be a problem.

Trumbull Mountain had done all the research about eBay and learned about the sales potential of Sunday nights. Therefore, when they began listing items, all the auctions ended on Sunday night. For the first few weeks, the company's eBay manager would check e-mails religiously every Sunday afternoon and evening. Answering e-mails became a full-time job and required much more time than she could squeeze into Sunday nights. Trumbull Mountain spread out the auctions to end at different points

sTrategy sNippet

Trumbull Mountain has settled on using the three-day auction format as it allows them to squeeze more auctions into a week and gives their items the least "middle-of-the-run" slump days as possible. Their auctions are seen well when they are newly listed, they have one mediocre traffic day, and then the traffic picks up again as the auction closes. This three-day method maximizes their "traffic-to-days-running" ratio for each of their auctions.

during the week. They found that their items still sold, and the workload was much easier to handle. Now they try to have auctions ending throughout the week.

dEscriptions

Unlike the restrictive listing title field, the listing description field is a wide-open canvas. The description field has no character limit and allows for the use of plain text, HTML, and some JavaScript. If you're an HTML guru, you will have fun coding the look and layout of your listing pages. However, if you're unfamiliar with the ways of the web designer, you needn't worry. There are many alternative ways to create attractive and effective listing pages.

The "description" box is somewhat of a misnomer. Yes, it is where you should describe your item, but you will need to use it for so much more than merely description that it should be named something more weighty, like the "listing advertisement page" box.

While the description box allows for simple plain text descriptions, you should never settle for the ugliness and confines of plain text formatting. You run a professional business and therefore need to represent your business professionally. There are several ways to accomplish this.

Your Listing Template

Hiring a professional web designer to create a stock listing template for you is your best move. Your listing page should be attractive, customized, and consistent across all of your item listings. To accomplish this correctly, you will need the help of someone familiar with HTML, JavaScript, and image editing. The final template will need to be inserted into your eBay management software as your "ad template," "listing template," "auction template," or whatever your program chooses to call it. Doing this will allow you to create hundreds of listing pages quickly without needing to mess with your new template's HTML code.

When designing your template, be sure that it includes a link to your store, photo links to related items in your store, and links to various categories in your store, such as "Bargain Deals," "New Items," and "The Most Expensive Things We Sell." Your item listings pages should be advertisements not only for the specific items they're representing, but also for the rest of your eBay operation. Your auction and Fixed Price listings should serve as hooks in the auction stream, pulling people into your store where profits per sale are guaranteed. By placing links and promotional boxes into your original listing template, you make promoting yourself in every listing much easier.

If you cannot hire a professional designer, you should turn next to your eBay management software. Many of the programs available have attractive templates built in. These, of course, will not be customized to your company, but they will be a far cry from black text on a white background.

Aside from the sheer attractiveness and professionalism of using a custom template, you will also gain the benefit of being able to use an unlimited number of pictures for free. By designing your template in HTML, you are able to insert as many photos as you would like as long as those photos are placed somewhere on your own web server. (See Chapter 5, Photography, for more.) Your eBay management program will help you insert photos into your template.

Your descriptions will be the face of your business on eBay. The customization you do in your eBay Store will help, but your listing description template is what most buyers will see. In every description for every item you should list your contact information—with the exception of your web address, which eBay does not allow. This instills buyers with the confidence that they can speak to a person should the transaction go awry.

Item Specifics

Your descriptions should also include every possible detail about the item that you can muster: size, color, weight, dimensions, manufacturer, history, condition, specific flaws, uses, model number, model year, number in set, included pieces, and so on. Your descriptions should be exhaustive. Spending as much time as you can painstakingly detailing every nuance and facet of your items will save you time down the road when you have fewer questions from buyers to answer.

The photos you choose to include should highlight every asset and detail every flaw of each item. The buyer needs to be able to accurately judge the value of the item so that he or she doesn't feel slighted when the item arrives. Photos also ensure that you receive the appropriate price. Try not to under-, or over-sell, your items. Be objective.

eBay Stores

an eBay Store is a great addition to your selling arsenal. A store will provide you with a space within eBay's huge ecosphere where your prices are fixed, customization is easy, and your competition isn't welcome. Don't think of your eBay Store as your business's niche from which you serve eBay's existing traffic. Think of your store as a doorway into the eBay universe. eBay's established traffic is huge, but it still pales in comparison to the larger shopping population of the Internet. Your auctions and Fixed-Price listings are confined to catering to the shoppers that are already on eBay, but your store has the potential to reach out beyond eBay's borders and pull in new buyers. When you design your store, don't limit yourself to eBay by considering only the needs and expectations of eBay shoppers. Instead, plan to appeal to a much larger audience—the whole Internet shopping population.

An eBay Store will provide you with many benefits. Not only will it increase your professional appearance and credibility on eBay, it will also make the more advanced marketing strategies possible, which I'll cover in Chapter 10, Marketing Strategies.

Store items have fixed prices. This provides you with two primary benefits. First, you can guarantee the profitability of every sale—something that can be tricky with auctions. Second, shoppers have more traditional price expectations once they enter a seller's eBay Store—especially if they are entering your store from somewhere other than eBay's auction stream. Because prices are fixed, the buyers are no longer offended by retail, or near-retail, prices. They see higher prices as an assurance of quality and good service. High prices are no longer an indicator that the buyer is getting ripped off—nor do they suggest that the buyer has succumbed to the competitive auction environment. Buyers become shoppers again, not bargain hunters. This presents a great opportunity for you to list and sell your items for full price, just as you would through your retail store.

This chapter will show you the main benefits of running an eBay Store and help you to build the most effective store possible.

oPtions

eBay offers three levels of the Stores program: Basic, Featured, and Anchor. The basic eBay Store is only $15.95 per month and comes with many of the important bells and whistles that the two more expensive subscription levels offer. The difference in pricing is mainly due to the level of automatic promotion you will receive and the placement of your store within eBay's store directories. Featured stores—$49.95 per month—receive a promotional text link within a list of the other featured stores. This list runs down the center of the eBay Stores gateway page. Links are also placed in the "Shop eBay Stores" box that appears on eBay's main search results pages. Anchor stores are quite a bit more expensive at $499.95 per month, but they are granted 24-hour dedicated customer support, frequent promotion in the "Shop eBay Stores" box, and a graphic advertisement at the top of the eBay Store gateway page—above the Featured Stores list.

For most users a basic store subscription will suffice, though I suggest opting for at least the Featured Store subscription as an early promotional boost while getting started.

gOals

Before you begin building and customizing your eBay Store, you should define some clear goals for your store. I caution you to not think too small during this step. Some sellers pack their eBay Store full of the items that they can't seem to sell successfully at auction. These sellers figure that because the listing fees are lower for store items, this is a good way to keep them available online without spending too much on eBay's auction listing fees. While this may be true, it is also thinking too small. Your eBay Store has huge potential. It is a full service e-commerce solution plunked right down in the middle of millions of shoppers. Search engines such as Google, Yahoo!, Live.com, Ask.com, and others drive traffic into eBay Stores every day. Popular shopping sites, such as Froogle, Shopping.com, and Honesty.com do the same. You should set ambitious goals for your eBay Store. The opportunities are endless.

The first goal of your eBay Store should be to reflect your existing business well. You should have a customized design that incorporates and boosts your company's branding. Your logo should be prominently displayed on your store. Your company colors should be obvious. Your contact information should be displayed everywhere you can fit it. You should set up your eBay Store exactly as you would set up any non-eBay e-commerce store. eBay shoppers are so accustomed to seeing eBay Stores that have been built using the boring default template and color scheme that when they see some actual design and customization of a store, it leaves an extremely favorable impression. Traffic coming to your store from off eBay will be expecting to see some graphic design and may find eBay's default laundry list of items a bit jarring. Professional design is as important here as it is for your main web site.

hElpful hInt

Trumbull Mountain put in a lot of time and effort to make their eBay Store stand out from the crowd. They designed a custom welcome page, along with several informational pages using a uniform header and menu bar. This helps customers move around the site just as they would on any non-eBay e-commerce site. Visit their store, along with the others listed below, to find some wonderful examples of store owners going the extra aesthetic mile. (See photos on next page.)

This seller has been quite successful using eBay's default store template and colors (not visible here).

Trumbull Mountain's customized welcome page greets newcomers with a pleasing design—a real asset when welcoming buyers from outside eBay.

Trumbull Mountain Tack Shop: http://stores.ebay.com/
Trumbull-Mountain-Tack-Shop
Blue Star Computers: http://stores.ebay.com/Blue-Star-Computer-Corp
Novica: http://stores.ebay.com/NOVICA-Store
JayCs Golf: http://stores.ebay.com/JayCsGolf
Groovy Geeks: http://stores.ebay.com/GroovyGeeks

Unless you're a web design whiz, I suggest you contact a professional web design firm that offers eBay Store design services, such as PIX-CLINIC (winner of the 2004 eBay Stores Design Award), proimpulse, or my web design and development company, Fruition Web Systems (www.fruition.ws).

The second goal of your eBay Store should be to encourage repeat traffic. Blue Star Computers does 95% of its eBay sales through its store. The majority of those sales are from repeat customers. Blue Star has proven themselves to be friendly, fast, and accurate. Their store is so well-stocked, and their service is so reliable, that their customers have no reason to shop the rest of eBay for better deals or better service. Instead, buyers just come right back to Blue Star's store where they know they'll find both.

Your aim should be to create a store that gives your customers no reason to shop elsewhere. To do this your store must be easy to use, helpful to the specific needs of your customers, and well-stocked with items at fair prices. In an effort to address the specific needs of their customers, Trumbull Mountain has posted helpful articles written by their knowledgeable staff. These articles address proper saddle fitting, saddle terminology, and an explanation of the store's unique saddle trial ride policy. Anticipate the needs of your customers and provide help in as many ways as you can. If a browsing customer finds your store to be more informative, more attractive, and easier to use than any of the other stores they've come across, you'll be the first seller they think of when they return to make a purchase.

The final goal of your eBay Store should be to pull in traffic from beyond eBay. With your unique design, your helpful tools, your informative articles, and eBay's full-service sales platform, there's no reason you shouldn't be promoting your eBay Store to every corner of the Internet. People all over the world are aware of eBay. It is an asset to you. Buyers know and trust eBay with their sensitive credit card information. Often buyers are skeptical of submitting personal information to the mom and pop e-commerce shops that are trying to make it independently on the Internet. eBay gives your buyers a level of protection and instant familiarity.

A custom-designed welcome page goes a long way toward making shoppers who might be unfamiliar with eBay feel welcome. As mentioned above, eBay's default store template shows a long list of all your store items as your welcome page. No independent e-commerce store would ever think to design a welcome page in this way. Shoppers are not used to seeing it—they want to see something more professional before they lay down their cash. The design rules that apply on the Internet at large apply to your eBay Store as well.

Your store's design and helpful tips should not stop at your welcome page. Each store item listing page needs to be considered for both regular customers and new buyers. Include the usual eBay information for the regular customers: shipping policies, return policies, accepted forms of payment, and so on. But also include a little hand-holding for buyers who might have found you through Froogle, Yahoo!, or another shopping site and aren't familiar with eBay. Include a blurb for these buyers that walks them through the checkout process. Explain to them what PayPal is, and that they do not need a PayPal account to use the service.

The best thing you can do to help both eBay veterans and newbies is to provide your telephone number, e-mail address, photos of your location, and some company history. Shoppers new to eBay are used to dealing directly with businesses, not through intermediaries like eBay. They don't understand what all the colorful stars mean and put no stock in "PowerSeller" banners or Store icons. Providing them with proof that your products are indeed from a legitimate business will make them feel better about making the final click. eBay veterans will appreciate having the assurance that your background and contact information provides as well—especially in the early days of your store when your feedback rating isn't yet off-the-charts impressive.

CUstomization

If you'd like to make a go at customizing your eBay Store yourself—
and I suggest you become familiar with this process even if you aren't
planning to take it on—you can do so through your "Manage My
Store" control panel.

There are several places where you can make customizations to your
store. Under the Store Design menu you have access to a number of setup and customization tools. Clicking Display Settings will present you
with basic customization options such as logo selection, store name,
theme, optional informational boxes, and header settings. The Store
Categories link will take you to your category manager where you can
create your own product categories and subcategories. The Promotional
Boxes link will help you to create and define special boxes that can run
along the top or the sides of your store pages. eBay provides a few premade boxes with standard tools or information, but they also allow you
to create your own boxes with your own text or HTML.

The real meat of the customization process takes place in the
Custom Pages manager. Here you can either use eBay's templates to create precut "custom" pages, or you can supply your own text or HTML.
You are limited to a certain number of custom pages, depending on
your subscription level. It is also in this manager that you can select to
use eBay's standard welcome page, or one of your own custom pages. I
suggest you create your own welcome page and designate it here.

The second important customization is of your store's header.
Under the Display Settings manager you can add information to your
store's header. This can be a good place to insert a simple menu linking
various store categories or items or custom pages. Customizing your
header gives you a good opportunity to do some extra promotion while
differentiating your store from all the other template-based stores.

eBay also allows you to specify search engine keywords with the
idea that the keywords you enter will help you to be found on Google,
Yahoo!, and other major non-eBay search engines. And finally eBay
provides an HTML builder where you can create code for store links
that can be cut and pasted into your custom pages, and header.

mArketing yOur sTore

Within your store manager, eBay provides access to some handy marketing tools, some of which can be tricky to figure out at first.

The easiest to understand is the mailing list manager. By placing the premade newsletter subscription promotional box on your store somewhere, you can begin collecting e-mail addresses from interested shoppers. You have the ability to create several e-mail mailing lists, which you can arrange in any manner you choose: by item category, by type of store promotion, and the like. I suggest setting up one general "Store Newsletter" mailing list at first to gauge your customers' interest. If you find that a lot of your shoppers are signing up, you may wish to expand your mailing list offerings, though in the beginning days of your store, subscriptions will only trickle in, and it saves time to have all your interested folks on one list.

Once you have a few subscribers, or an important promotion coming up, you should test out your new mailing list by sending out a promotional e-mail. You'll have some advanced formatting tools and optional promotional boxes available. Make use of all the space eBay allows to promote your items and categories. Sending these e-mails can be so much fun that it becomes addictive. Be careful not to abuse your privilege to e-mail your buyers. As you know, people do not give out their e-mail addresses lightly. If you bother your buyers with far-too-frequent e-mails, they will unsubscribe. E-mail responsibly.

In addition to digital promotion, you should consider printed promotions as well. Every time you send off a shipment, you have the opportunity to do some more, very inexpensive, promotion to a confirmed buyer. Including a print-out advertisement into each box you ship is a great way to promote your brand, improve customer communication, and sell more items. To make this task easier, eBay is thoughtful enough to provide the nifty "Promotional Flyer" tool. You simply select the promotions you would like to include on the flyer and click "Print." While helpful, this tool does have a difficult time formatting its dimensions to fit conveniently onto one sheet of 8½x11 paper. Admittedly, perfect formatting with HTML is incredibly difficult to achieve since nearly every computer will have a unique combination of operating system, web browser, printer software, and printer. You'll have to play around with the layout of your flyer to find the combination that fits best.

The most mystifying, but most potent, promotional tools that eBay offers Store owners are the Listing Feeds. "Feed" is a fancy name for an Internet-accessible file that is automatically updated by some sort of software at regular intervals or upon request. These files are sometimes referred to as RSS feeds, Atom Feeds, or XML feeds. In this instance, your listing feed is an XML file containing information about all the items in your store. This file is automatically updated when you create or remove item listings. These files are referred to as "Feeds" because the programs people use to access these files—feed readers—are directed to the web address where these files reside and the programs monitor them constantly for updates—creating the illusion of constantly streaming information through a "feed."

The most basic use for your listing feed is to subscribe to it yourself via your web browser bookmark utility, your Google Homepage, or your My Yahoo! page. This would allow you to monitor your store's listings without logging onto eBay. There are many applications that make use of feeds: screen-savers, auction monitors, web browsers, and e-mail clients. You can even send your eBay Store listing feed to your main business web site where you can display always up-to-date store listing information, automatically. And therein lies your listing feed's largest potential: publishing to other web sites.

By sending your listing feed to larger services, such as Google Base, you can include all the items in your store in millions of other product searches across the Internet. eBay even provides you with a specially formatted version of your listing feed for Google Base, which will list your store items in searches from Google and Froogle. In addition to Google Base, you can submit your store item feed to Yahoo! Search Marketing, Shopzilla, Smarter, AddMe.com, and more. Search the Internet for "submit product feed" or "submit item feed." You will find several places that are looking to include your items in their search results. Some services will ask for a submission fee. Investigate pay services thoroughly before signing up.

The beauty of submitting your listing feed is that for a few hours of work you can increase the exposure of your items by millions of people. And, since your listing feed file is updated automatically by eBay, it will only require minimal work on your part every few weeks to make sure your items remain listed on the various shopping services where you submitted them.

To make it even easier for you to publish your items to the various Google search engines, Google has published Google Base Store Connector. This is a download application for Windows PCs that will check your store listing feed for changes, format it into Google Base-approved format, and then upload it to Google Base automatically. It is a free download and makes it simple to publish your items on Google every month.

To best capitalize on the new non-eBay traffic to your new store, you should consider taking extra steps to make it easier for your off-eBay traffic to reach your store. The web address that eBay assigns your store could be worse, but it could be better too.

One solution is to register a top-level domain name that can be pointed to your eBay store. For example: **www.MonitorMonster.com** is much easier to remember than **http://stores.ebay.com/The-Monitor-Monster-Store**. By registering a domain name for your eBay Store you can make it even easier for off-eBay traffic to find.

However, if your eBay Store is your primary online selling solution, registering another domain name just for your eBay Store may confuse your current customers. In lieu of registering another domain name for your business, consider creating a redirect page as an extension of your existing web site. Trumbull Mountain has set up **www.trumbullmtn.com/ebay** as an easy-to-remember address that redirects visitors instantly and automatically to their eBay Store.

There are many reasons to promote your store beyond eBay's marketplace. The first, obviously, is to bring in more customers. The second is to direct traffic past your competition. Consider that your customers who have found you from eBay searches have selected you from among all your eBay competition. However, when customers come to you from a source external to eBay, they are linked directly to you and your items. They do not see your eBay competition. This is a feat that cannot be accomplished through auction links, Fixed-Price listing promotions, and other on-eBay marketing strategies.

bEyond eBay

Some online shoppers avoid eBay. They either find it a dauntingly large world to enter, or prefer the traditional Amazon.com style of shopping online. In order to capture the largest audience for your products available, you will need to toss out the largest net, and this means setting up an e-commerce store outside of eBay.

You may be rolling your eyes at this point at the suggestion that you open yet another store. You already have auctions to deal with, and fixed-price listings, and your eBay Store inventory—not to mention your *actual* store. If you think that's too much to juggle, I would agree with you.

For sellers looking to establish eBay as a profitable and sizable sales channel for their business, there's only one non-eBay e-commerce store solution I recommend—and that's because it's from eBay.

eBay's ProStores service enables online sellers to set up a complete, customizable, and independent store online. The system is based on technology developed by a company called Kurant. The system, originally named StoreSense, has been earning high praise from many various Internet review magazines since its launch in 1998. eBay acquired Kurant, along with StoreSense, in late 2005. eBay renamed the service ProStores and began integrating Kurant's system into their own. Today, ProStores is the only online selling service that allows sellers to manage their eBay listings, and external sales listings, from one location. It makes the task of running two independent online sales channels manageable for small businesses. It is the extensive integration between this independent selling platform, your eBay operation, and your PayPal account, that will really save you time and money.

Subscribers to the ProStores service can leverage the system's eBay integration to post their ProStores items on eBay and their eBay items in their ProStores store. Through the provided management tools, subscribers can manage their entire ProStores operation, along with their eBay payments, shipping, inventory, and listings. The integration between the two selling systems is excellent and improving with every new version of ProStores.

It is important to note that your ProStore is not like an off-eBay version of your eBay Store. Your ProStore uses different management tools, inventory tracking, checkout system, and so on—which is often an advantage. eBay has not simply copied their eBay Stores platform over to ProStores, it has taken Kurant's award-winning platform and integrated it into eBay's marketplace.

Your ProStore is entirely customizable. You can use one of their 180 design templates, use their store design utility, or entirely provide your own HTML code. Your ProStore can be located at any top-level domain name (**www.mystore.com**) or as a subdomain of the ProStores URL (**https://store02.prostores.com/mystore**). You are provided 200 e-mail accounts, up to 20 GB of storage space, up to 400 GB of data transfer capacity per month, access to e-mail marketing tools, sales reports, traffic reports, complete secure checkout, credit card payment processor integration, shopping carts, and more. This service is not designed to compliment your eBay sales, it is intended to stand on its own—which it accomplishes very well.

Not only is your ProStore easy to manage in itself, but also it provides some options that actually make running your eBay Store a little easier as well. For example, ProStores will automatically (if asked) redirect your eBay buyers to your ProStores checkout system so that you can manage all your online sales through one interface and one reporting system. ProStores also automatically submits your product list feed to large comparison shopping web sites such as Froogle, Shopping.com, Shopzilla, and so on. Your eBay Store will not do this for you automatically.

ProStores also provide a robust inventory manager. At its highest level of service ProStores will even manage your product supply chain by alerting vendors when drop-shipments are required, listing a virtual inventory for to-be-received items, and more.

As with your eBay Store, aesthetic design is important. ProStores understands this fact. They have provided 180 premade templates from which store owners can choose. They are, in general, boring and unattractive. Your customers will want to see more from you, and therefore I suggest you take advantage of your ProStore's full HTML customization option. This is where you will need to reenlist the help of your favorite web designer. Make sure you use a similar, if not identical, design to your eBay Store and eBay listings. This will create a brand continuity across your various sales channels that won't go unnoticed by your customers.

If you have yet to find a favorite web designer, ProStores offers design services. Here you are guaranteed to find talented designers who are aware of every nook and cranny of the ProStores service. They will help you push the customization of your store to the limits of what's possible.

A ProStores store will cost you between $6.95/month for their Express service and $249.95/month for their Enterprise service. Express customers are charged 1.5% of every sale, and the other three plans are charged 0.5% per sale. Also, eBay Stores subscribers receive a 30% discount on their monthly ProStores fees.

If you don't have an external e-commerce solution, this can be a great way to get one started cheap. And if you already have an e-commerce solution up and running, the built-in marketing features, full customization, and eBay integration that ProStores offers may lead you to consider ditching your current e-commerce setup.

Payments

When a customer shops in your retail store, they hand you cash and walk out. When they shop on your web site, they give you a credit card number and log off. The money moves directly from them to you. After operating an established retail business, you may not be accustomed to selling through intermediaries like eBay. The fact that eBay acts as a bridge between sellers and buyers often leads to some misconceptions as to how the actual transaction takes place. One of the questions I'm most often asked about selling on eBay is: Yeah ... but, how do I get paid?

Contrary to the common misconception, eBay remains largely absent from the monetary transactions between buyers and sellers. Most often, buyers pay sellers directly using a variety of methods. Receiving personal checks, money orders, cashier's checks, credit card numbers, and all the conventional means of collecting payment are still very much in use. The only time eBay is involved in a financial transaction is when the buyer chooses to pay through PayPal, eBay's online transaction service.

pAypAl

When eBay first launched, the company was never involved in the transfer of money between buyers and sellers. They stayed as far away from buyer/seller financial transactions and disputes as possible. The company handled no escrow money, they held no inventory, they simply ran a web site and charged a listing fee. This kept their expenses low and their business extremely profitable.

Over time, buyers and sellers needed a better way to transfer money easily online. Sending checks and money orders through the mail was no longer fast enough. Wire transfers were too much of a hassle for both buyer and seller to be feasible. The need for an easy way for sellers to instantly collect funds became obvious. In May of 1999, eBay made an attempt to fill the gap by purchasing Billpoint, a young online transaction company. BillPoint's services were then truncated to allow only for the payment of eBay auctions. eBay renamed BillPoint "eBay Payments."

Though the new eBay Payments service made it easier for buyers and sellers to exchange money online, by February of 2000, it was overwhelmingly obvious that eBay users preferred the payment services of a small company named PayPal over eBay's service—by a margin of roughly 50 to 1. Just two months later, PayPal was the promoted payment service on over 1,000,000 auctions.

PayPal grew exponentially over the next few years—so much so that eBay came to realize that their eBay Payments service would never fly as long as PayPal was around. eBay began to discourage users from using PayPal, to which PayPal retaliated by filing an anticompetition complaint against eBay. In October of 2002, eBay purchased PayPal outright and integrated the financial company's services into its own. The eBay Payments service that began as BillPoint was phased out of use.

Today, PayPal is the standard method of payment on eBay. Nearly every seller accepts PayPal payments, and millions of buyers choose to use it. PayPal is becoming the preferred payment service of users across the Internet—not just eBay members.

Since its acquisition by eBay, PayPal has been expanding in earnest. They now operate in 13 countries, conduct transactions in 17 currencies, and manage over 123 million user accounts. They offer debit cards, credit cards, money market accounts, and a new virtual debit card service aimed at making it easier and more secure to spend money online.

PayPal makes transferring funds over the Internet incredibly easy. They claim to enable people to send money to anybody with an e-mail account. This is technically true, but also misleading in that the recipient must register for a PayPal account by providing bank and credit card information before being able to claim the payment. Many users find the requirement of supplying bank information annoying, but it is a necessary security measure that PayPal takes to confirm the user's identity.

How PayPal Works

PayPal accounts work similarly to any conventional bank account. Users have balance accounts that they can use to deposit and withdraw funds. Sending money to other PayPal users is as easy as specifying the person's PayPal-registered e-mail address on PayPal's web site and clicking a button. PayPal simply moves the money into the recipient's account, from where they can then withdraw into their local bank accounts. It is this extremely easy-to-use system that makes PayPal a very attractive method to pay for items purchased on eBay. In the early days of PayPal on eBay, sellers needed only to post their PayPal-registered e-mail address, and buyers could instantly send them the money. Today, you will find that eBay has integrated PayPal much more intricately into their selling platform.

If you register for a PayPal account, and specify in your eBay account settings that you would like to offer your buyers the option of paying through PayPal, eBay will automatically send your buyers a "Pay Now" link in their winner's notification e-mail that directs them to a custom-made PayPal invoice. The buyer simply signs into their PayPal account, clicks Pay, and the transaction is complete. You receive the funds instantly.

If your buyers do not have, and do not want to register for, a PayPal account, they are now in luck. Recently PayPal created a system that allows buyers to submit payments through PayPal's service using their MasterCard, Visa, American Express, or Discover credit card without requiring them to register for a PayPal account. This feature essentially provides sellers with an inexpensive credit card merchant account and payment processor. Buyers enjoy being able to submit payment without being asked to register.

Many eBay shoppers prefer to use PayPal simply for its convenience. But others prefer to use it because it keeps their financial information safe. PayPal does not send a buyer's credit card or banking information to the seller. Instead, it keeps the buyer's financial information private and handles the transaction on its own. Buyers like knowing that their sensitive financial information is kept with the company they trust and not being strewn around the Internet to sellers, shops, and possibly nefarious scam artists.

PayPal is free for buyers, but sellers are charged a fee per transaction. (See Appendix A for PayPal fees.) This frees sellers from paying the high monthly and transaction fees associated with traditional e-commerce merchant accounts.

Inside your PayPal account you will find many tools to help you track and manage your eBay transactions. In addition to a detailed history of every transaction, you will find shipping utilities, payment refund capabilities, money market incentives, payment notifications, web site integration utilities, and more. PayPal, in itself, is a robust service that many sellers find to be useful beyond their eBay transactions.

As you'll learn as you research PayPal further, not all eBay sellers enjoy the service. The per-transaction fees PayPal charges are not insignificant when conducting hundreds or thousands of eBay transactions per month. Also, PayPal's fees are deducted from the item's final selling price at the end of a parade of other deducted selling fees such as eBay's listing fee and the final value fee. Sellers can get discouraged watching their final selling prices disintegrate.

Also, as much as your PayPal account functions like a normal bank account, PayPal is not a bank. Your funds are not FDIC insured.

Any money you leave sitting in your PayPal account could very well vanish if PayPal goes out of business. This is important to keep in mind when your sales begin rolling in and your PayPal account begins reaching amounts beyond 10 or 20 thousand dollars.

For a time, PayPal offered an AutoSweep function that would automatically initiate a withdrawal of all your PayPal funds to your local bank account on a schedule you could set. They discontinued their service in an attempt to encourage people to keep money in their accounts. This was a step backwards in my opinion, as it was a move away from their customers' best interests.

PayPal is extremely vigilant about preventing fraud. You may have noticed this already—and if you haven't you soon will—but PayPal is one of the most targeted Internet financial services by spammers, phishers, and identity thieves. eBay sellers receive spoof e-mails every day posing as correspondence from PayPal. These e-mails look identical to the e-mails that PayPal itself actually does send, but they contain completely fraudulent information and spurious web links. In time you will learn to identify these e-mails from other e-mails, but they serve as a constant reminder to PayPal that it must take serious steps to protect its customers.

Sometimes the serious steps taken by PayPal to protect customers are made in error. They have been known to freeze accounts containing large sums of money for what they deem to be suspicious activity. Users with frozen accounts find it difficult, if not impossible, to get a clear explanation as to the reason the funds were frozen and when they will be made available again.

In general, PayPal is unfortunately difficult to get in contact with. Customer support is seriously lacking and has not improved since eBay's acquisition. For this, and the reasons stated above, I always suggest that sellers make it a habit to clear out their PayPal accounts every few days. You don't want to become one of the businesses crippled by a frozen cash flow.

In spite of it being an imperfect service, I suggest that you do register for a PayPal account and offer their payment services to your buyers. I have been using my PayPal account trouble-free for over five years now, and I have yet to run into anyone personally who has any serious trouble with the service. Don't let the tales of woe scare you, but be aware of the risk of keeping large sums of money in a nonin-sured account at a company that's difficult to contact.

mAking pAyments eAsier

Biz Parris of West Barnstable Trading Company runs a simple operation. She does not accept credit cards, has a cash box in the back room to handle sales, and when she's unavailable to tend to a customer waiting to pay, she'll simply call out, "Just put the money down anywhere. I'll find it. Thank you."

For a time, years ago, she accepted credit cards at her store. She found it to be a nuisance as it disrupted her cash flow and was compli-cated to figure into her monthly accounting. The deal breaker came when she was involved with a dispute with a fraudulent buyer. The credit card company did not go to bat for her and she lost out on a few thousand dollars. She packed up the credit card terminal and hasn't looked back.

PayPal, however, Biz finds to be "very viable." She uses it every day, and on every auction, without hesitation. It even allows her to accept credit cards at her store again. If a customer can't pay in cash, Biz sits them down at her computer and asks them to submit payment to her through PayPal with any major credit or debit card. The whole process takes only a few minutes longer than it would with the old credit card machine, and both Biz and the customer are satisfied.

To register for a PayPal account, visit **www.paypal.com**. You will need to register for a Business Account to make use of the advanced selling options. You will be asked for your credit card information, your bank's routing number, and your bank account's account num-ber. These can be scary to give out, but are necessary for PayPal to be able to transfer funds into your local account. Upon registration, PayPal will make two small deposits to your local account, the amounts of which you will need to verify to confirm that your account is working properly. This process can take a few days. During that time, poke around PayPal's options and settings. You will want to set up your addresses, eBay integration options, and customization fea-tures before you begin collecting payments from buyers.

For sellers who have experienced problems with PayPal in the past, or who just don't want to pay the extra fees, there are thankfully other options for collecting payment. eBay is an open marketplace and does not lock any sellers into using their own payment service. In the absence of, or in addition to, PayPal you should also accept other forms of payment. You'll find that some buyers refuse to use PayPal and need another way to send you money. The more methods of payment you accept, the easier it will be for you to sell your items.

cRedit cArds

There are several secure ways for you to accept credit cards for your eBay sales without the need for PayPal. If you already accept credit cards in your retail location, this can be a good way to keep your sales and accounting from changing too much after the addition of eBay.

The primary concern with accepting credit cards over the Internet must be security, both for you and your customer. Technologies exist that enable you to build, or pay a company to build, a custom checkout process that will securely transfer credit card information to you. If you already have an custom e-commerce site, then you have this ability already. If you prefer not to bother with using, or building, your own checkout process, there are several premade solutions available to you. In fact, most eBay management services, such as Andale, ChannelAdvisor Pro, and Terapeak offer customizable checkout services that allow you to accept credit cards—either through their, or your own, payment processor.

There are many advantages to building your own checkout solution. First, it bolsters your company's professionalism. Buyers like to see that you have your act together. If you are able to transfer buyers from eBay to a checkout system on your company's web site, they will feel safer inserting their credit card information and be impressed with your serious commitment to selling on eBay. Buyers who choose to use external checkout systems are usually bounced around the Internet from random payment service to payment service. They will appreciate that when purchasing a new mobile phone on eBay from NortheastWireless, they are transferred to NotheastWireless's web site to make payment. Such continuity is rare on eBay.

Building trust on eBay is paramount to success. Buyers trust eBay, and after your feedback rating is high enough, they will trust you. However, shopping online is always a risky proposition and online shoppers are justifiably a skittish bunch. If you give them any reason to doubt the legitimacy of a transaction, they simply will cancel the sale.

Therefore it is in your best interest to create continuity for your buyers. Often this is just a matter of making simple aesthetic choices: your logo on eBay should match the logo on your web site, your color schemes should be similar, your contact information should be consistent across all pages and web sites.

But sometimes creating continuity over the course of a transaction requires more effort on your part. For example, many eBay management services offer their own external checkout service, which helps their sellers manage sales and accept credit cards. This can be a real help to sellers, but, if implemented incorrectly, transferring buyers off eBay to submit payment information can hurt sales. When buyers see that they've been transferred to an unfamiliar web address, they become suspicious of foul play.

Pretend for a moment that you are your buyer. You receive dozens of fraudulent e-mails per day posing to be from eBay and PayPal and countless other financial institutions. Each of these e-mails you receive contains a link to an unfamiliar web address that asks for your financial information. You have rightly learned to be suspicious of every unfamiliar web address that requests financial information. So why then, as a buyer, would it ever seem like a good idea when shopping on eBay to supply your financial information to an unfamiliar web site? It goes against every Internet instinct a buyer has. But this is precisely what many eBay sellers ask their buyers to do.

When shopping with you on eBay, your buyer is aware of, and willing to trust, two companies: yours and eBay. They are wholly unaware of the eBay management service you use—as they should be—and have likely never heard of it before. They have no reason to trust it. Let's say, for example, that you've chosen ChannelAdvisor Pro to help you manage your auctions. This is a quality service and you would do well to choose it. They provide you with a checkout system and invite buyers to use this checkout system by placing a link on each of your auction pages. Upon completion of the auction, your winning buyer clicks the "Checkout" link that you've placed on your auction page. They are then redirected to a web site with an address similar to http://chnla.com/r.asp?z=4&p=616847654&a=364684412.

This likely sets off all sorts of alarms for your buyers. The main URL "chnla.com" means nothing to them, and certainly looks suspicious. A more conventional URL such as "channelcheckout.com" or "marketplacesales.com" would have a better chance of being more readily trusted by buyers, but the simple fact that they've been redirected away from eBay and not to your web site is enough to startle any buyer away from a sale. The buyer would not blink twice, however, if, after being redirected away from eBay to purchase a hat from Sally's Hat Rack, they were sent to "SallysHatRack.com."

Integrating eBay checkout into your own web site can be expensive, but it will increase your sell-through rate by more than enough to cover the cost. You can find capable programmers to help build you an eBay checkout system by searching in eBay's Solutions Directory, or doing a search on Google. To find local programmers, you can ask your local chamber of commerce for help.

hElpful hInt

There are a few safety precautions that must be taken when building your own eBay checkout system. Here are a few rules to follow.

Never, never, never request that customers send credit card information over e-mail. When an e-mail message leaves its source it begins a journey across the Internet, bouncing from computer to computer. Some e-mails pass through hundreds of computers before reaching the final destination. At any of those hops along the way, an e-mail can be read by a curious and malicious system administrator, hacker, or even by e-mail-scanning software. If the programmers you've found to build the system suggest that you receive sensitive sales information via e-mail, thank them for their time and show them the door. They obviously have no clue about system security.

Any secure checkout system must use SSL (Secure Socket Layering) encryption to protect the entire system. It isn't enough to simply encrypt the checkout pages that a buyer uses to input their credit card information, the system must also encrypt the administration pages that transmit the credit card numbers to you. Unencrypted data can be read by third parties whenever it travels from the Internet to your computer.

The price for this type of checkout system can range anywhere from $2,500 to $6,000, depending on the included features. If you've been quoted more than that, you should request a detailed explanation of each proposed feature and how it relates to the total cost. If you've been quoted less than that, you may end up with a shoddy system that puts you and your customers in danger. This is not an area of your business where you can afford to cut corners.

If you cannot invest in integrating your own checkout system into your web site, I suggest you make do with accepting credit cards through PayPal or asking your buyers to call you during business hours.

If your eBay management solution has made their external checkout system too alluring to resist, there are some steps you can take to minimize the damage caused using an unfamiliar web address. First, place a clear note in your auction pages that you use service XYZ for checkout processing and that the buyer will be redirected to web address XYZ.com for processing. Place this note at the very end of your item's description, as the link that is automatically placed on your auction pages will likely be placed just below that.

Second, make sure that the web address to which your buyers are redirected isn't inherently suspicious. ChannelAdvisor's checkout URL (chnla.com) is pretty bad as many of the spoofed e-mail messages originate in eastern Europe or Asia and point unsuspecting recipients to web addresses that end in .ch and .cn. Buyers who have been burned before in the past by one of these e-mails will no doubt be scared by the connotations of "chn." A good checkout address is one that uses actual words that state the web site's actual purpose. It needs to be extremely reassuring in order to overcome the buyer's suspicion of an unfamiliar web site.

And third, if you're inclined to make a complicated project out of it, you could register your own checkout domain name, such as "JoshsSportCheckout.com," host it with your web host as a "frame redirect," and then ask your local programmer to whip up a simple program that redirects traffic and information from JoshsSportCheckout.com to the checkout system from your eBay management service. With this in place, your buyers will see your new domain name in their address bar, but the checkout service in the browser window.

If you do opt to invest in building your own checkout system, there are a number of ways to process credit card numbers. First, and most simply, the system could be set up to only collect credit card and buyer address information. Once collected, you could log into your checkout system and read the credit card numbers from your browser. Then you would simply process these numbers in your store using your usual method for doing so. This is the more laborious method for processing credit card sales, but it will save you quite a bit of money every month because your bank will charge you an increased rate for accepting online sales.

The second, less time-consuming option is to build your checkout system to process credit card numbers instantly and automatically when it receives them. Your bank will be able to tell you, or the system's programmers, how to integrate your system with their payment processor. In the long run, this is the better choice. It will save you time every day, and if your sales grow to be hundreds per day or more, processing credit card numbers by hand will no longer be logistically feasible or cost-effective.

pErsonal cHecks, Cashier's Checks, and Money Orders

Even with all the high-tech and instant payment options available, some sellers still only accept paper forms of payment—and with good reason. Cashing a check or money order doesn't cost you anything. If your buyers mail you payment directly you can avoid PayPal fees, merchant account fees, payment processor fees, and so on. This is a slower way to do business, and there is more risk involved, but it can boost your profit per item significantly.

I don't suggest you limit your business to accepting only these slower forms of payment. Buyers will expect your business to accept electronic payments, and you will lose customers to your competition if you don't. But accepting these forms of payment in addition to one, or both, of the methods above can be beneficial.

Accepting a personal check from a customer standing in front of you can be risky; accepting a check through the mail is more so. Scams abound on the Internet and are prevalent on eBay as well. When accepting checks and money orders you need to take extra steps to protect yourself.

First off, you should never ship an item before the buyer's check or money order clears. This can make for some awkward days while both you and your buyer tap your fingers and stare at the ceiling and you wait for your bank to receive the funds, but it will pay off. In order to make those awkward days less annoying for your customers, you should state on your item pages that if the buyer elects to pay by check or money order, you will wait for the funds to clear before shipping. This way the buyer knows beforehand and won't ding you with negative feedback for slow shipping.

You must also be weary of counterfeit checks and money orders. Over the years many con artists have been very successful at duping eBay sellers out of money and goods with counterfeit money orders. And, as printing technology improves, so do the chances of counterfeiters at being successful. In all honesty, untrained professionals have little chance of detecting well-done fake checks or money orders, which is why it is so important to wait for the funds to actually clear in your bank before you send off an item.

Limiting your acceptance of checks and money orders to domestic sales can help you to minimize your risk since many of the scams perpetrated on eBay are done from overseas.

Also, use your common sense when confronted with suspicious requests. Often sellers on eBay will be asked to accept a check for an amount well above the item's value, and then send the remaining cash along with the shipment of the item. Obviously this is just an attempt by the buyer to lace their pockets with someone else's dough, but it works often enough on inexperienced sellers that scam artists keep trying it.

iNternational cOnsiderations

As I mentioned above, most scams on eBay originate from overseas. This could be because the fear of being caught is dramatically reduced by 15,000 miles, or because some goods are worth more in other parts of the world, but whatever the reason, conducting business overseas increases your risk of running into scams.

I would recommend dealing only with domestic sales if the honest international market weren't so huge and full of potential. eBay has auction sites operating in 26 countries around the world, many of them with large English-speaking populations. When you click the "Ship Worldwide" option while listing an item, you are selecting to automatically insert your item into 25 other eBay marketplaces—each with new markets and new potential. Your chances of making the sale increase drastically. You may discover a huge foreign market for your items that you never knew existed. Many sellers make incredible profits by purchasing cheap goods domestically, and then selling them on foreign eBay sites where those goods are rare and hard to come by. The best way to discover those markets for your items is to try your hand at shipping worldwide.

If you've ever stood in line at the post office to fill out customs forms you know that shipping across international borders can cost your business a lot of time and your buyer a lot of extra money. As the world shrinks, shipping companies such as DHL and FedEx are working to make international shipping less laborious. Pitney Bowes, the well-known shipping equipment company, offers a new service called ClearPath that handles all the trouble of international shipping for you.

If you are selling overseas, credit card payments become far more risky. The Internet is awash with unsuspecting people's credit card numbers that can turn up in anyone's hands anywhere in the world. Trumbull Mountain experienced some trouble with fraudulent credit card payments when they received an order for several saddles to be shipped to Japan, though the buyer was from New Jersey. The credit card was accepted, Trumbull Mountain got paid, and they therefore shipped the saddles off to Japan. The credit card, they learned, had been stolen. The saddles, payment, and shipping cost were gone forever. One of the best ways to protect your business and your goods from ending up on a shady loading dock halfway across the world is to limit your shipping to verified addresses. That is to say, limit your shipping to the address used on the provided form of payment. If the buyer is paying through PayPal, refuse to ship anywhere but to their verified PayPal address. If the buyer uses a credit card, use only the billing address associated with that card. This can become a troublesome policy for buyers around the holidays when they often prefer to ship gifts directly to friends and relatives, but it can save you a lot of frustration. I suggest you use this policy with no exceptions on international orders, and use your best judgment for domestic sales.

cOmmon sCams

The most common eBay scams target buyers. But that does not mean you should let your guard down. Buyers have figured out some interesting ways to get money, goods, and service from eBay sellers. To help you recognize these, and avoid being scammed, I've collected the most common scams of sellers here.

Cash Back

An Example: A buyer sends a seller a $1,000 money order for a $10 item. The buyer then apologizes for the error, insists that he needs the item right away, and to save time the seller should just throw the item in a box along with the remaining $990 dollars. Often the buyer will request that the money be sent to a location other than the item. The money order turns out to be a fake, and the overly gracious seller is robbed of the value of the item and $990.

How to Avoid: Avoiding this scam is pretty obvious. As a seller you should never accept "overpayments" and you should never—except in the case of legitimate refunds—send cash or checks back to buyers.

Defective/Missing Goods

An Example: A buyer legitimately purchases an item through any method of payment. The seller sends off the item to a verified mailing address. Upon the item's arrival, the buyer does one of two things: either he denies that the item has arrived, or claims that the item arrived badly damaged. In either case the buyer requests that a replacement be sent right away or a full refund be given.

How to Avoid: Avoiding being scammed in this instance can be difficult. Sometimes packages do become lost in the mail, and sometimes they do suffer damage. Using tracking on every item you ship will allow you to confirm delivery of packages and will enable you to hunt down the package should it go missing. Also, if a buyer claims that an item has been damaged in delivery, request that they ship the item back to you so that you can inspect it before sending a replacement or refund.

Fake Escrow

An Example: A buyer wins an auction and sends the seller an e-mail claiming that the money for the item has been placed into an escrow account and will be released to the seller upon shipment of the item. (Sometimes these e-mails will be made to appear to come from PayPal and will claim to have used PayPal's Escrow Service. There is no PayPal Escrow Service.) The seller ships the item, expecting payment to be released, but it never arrives.

How to Avoid: Never agree to use an escrow service. You should always have payment before you ship an item.

Credit Card Fraud

An Example: A buyer purchases an item legitimately from a seller. A few days later the buyer calls their credit card company and files a complaint about missing or damaged goods. The credit card company notifies you, or PayPal if the charge came through them, and withdraws the amount of the purchase from your account.

How to Avoid: Unfortunately, this one is hard to avoid. You can do everything right and still get hit with this one. The good news is that credit card companies are quite adept at catching scams before they get to you.

Scammed in Person

An Example: This scam works similarly to the Missing/Damaged Goods scam. A buyer legitimately purchases an items from a seller and pays through PayPal. The buyer requests to pick up the item from the seller's retail location, and does so. A few days later the buyer files a complaint with PayPal claiming that the item was never sent, and PayPal withdraws the money for the purchase from the seller's account. PayPal only accepts tracking information from a major delivery service as proof of delivery. There is nothing the seller can do to prove to PayPal that the item was picked up by the buyer.

How to Avoid: If a buyer requests to pick up an item from your retail location, ask them to pay at the time of pickup. Using PayPal for pickups can leave you with no recourse against this scam.

Fake Payment E-mail

An Example: A buyer wins an auction and sends the seller a fake "You've Received Payment" e-mail in the exact style of PayPal's usual e-mail. The seller, after receiving the e-mail, ships the item only to learn later that the e-mail had been forged and that no payment was made.

How to Avoid: Confirm each payment you receive through any payment service, whether it is PayPal or Western Union or your own checkout system, by logging into the appropriate service's system and verifying the payment independently from any e-mail you receive.

Listing Management

Once you've got the initial setup of your eBay operation squared away, managing your listings will become your most time-consuming daily task. I've run into businesses that manage to keep track of upwards of 10,000 item listings on eBay at any given time. Without the proper tools, it is possible to quickly and inadvertently list more items than can reasonably be managed by one small business. The key to becoming, and remaining, organized when it comes to the items you sell on eBay is to invest sufficient time in researching the tools that will best fit your business and eBay expansion.

Many businesses go through several listing management utilities or services before finding—or building—one that works well for their needs. You will need to spend the time and money necessary to work your way through the hundreds of various offerings available before you settle on just one. It is best to narrow your choices down to just a few possible utilities or services before you start listing any items on eBay at all. Once you begin selling, the other important tasks in your day— answering questions, shipping, photography—will eat up your time and make it even more difficult for you to do the necessary research.

Once you select a service or program, you will almost certainly wish it offered something it doesn't or worked in a way that it can't. A program or service is never really tested until it has been put to use for a few months. However, switching your eBay operation from one management tool to another is not a small job. Therefore it is best to make these switches early in your expansion when the number of listings you will need to move will be smallest.

There are hundreds of worthy listing management utilities and services available to you. They are changing, upgrading, appearing, and disappearing all the time. Therefore, profiling specific programs in this book would do you little good six months from now. Instead, this chapter will point out some key elements that a good eBay management program should have, some nonintuitive factors that should play into your decision, and some accessibility options you need to consider. Looking for these essential elements at the outset of your search could help you cut your research time in half.

eBay's tOols vs. tHird-pArty sOlutions

eBay believes that level competition in an open marketplace will produce the best prices, tools, and services. This belief drives them to keep their own marketplace open and equal for all sellers, and why the company opens up access to the back-end of their site to non-eBay software developers. It is in eBay's interest for its sellers to have the best tools with which to manage their eBay sales. Unlike many other platform owners on the Internet, eBay is humble enough to realize that the best tools may not always come from within their company. Therefore, they have built a robust API through which outside software developers can gain access to eBay's functions and databases. This API enables talented software developers of all sizes to create and distribute and sell their own unique eBay management tools.

These third-party developers have several advantages over eBay's developers. First, they're not bound to eBay's interface guidelines and are able to therefore create beautiful and (sometimes) intuitive user interfaces. Second, these developers have the freedom to create tools that not only integrate with eBay, but also with other marketplaces such as Yahoo!, Amazon, and Overstock. And finally, these developers are often made up of small, dedicated programming teams and therefore have an easier time releasing updates more frequently. This can be a huge advantage when security holes are discovered, when the competition unveils a useful tool, or when eBay updates their own programming code.

Third-party programs do have their share of disadvantages as well. As they are not privy to eBay's inner workings, they cannot know what eBay has planned for the future. eBay therefore has an advantage when aligning their software to instantly work perfectly with newly announced features and marketplaces. Third-party developers may be able to quickly produce an update to their own software to cope with the new features, but they'll never be able to beat eBay to the punch.

Second, third-party developers are small businesses in themselves. They are subject to all the trials of any small business. You may find that after six months of searching you've finally settled on one ultimate eBay management utility only to find out that the company had to shut its doors due to an accounting error. When using eBay's own tools, you can feel more certain that the software will be around and available for a long time.

When testing software you should consider not only the virtues of the program itself, but also the benefits and drawbacks of the development company. I suggest that you only use services from companies that have been around for a few years or more, and that you try out a few of their support lines (telephone, e-mail, chat) before you commit to just one provider.

d**Esktop** a**Pplication vs.** w**Eb-**b**Ased** u**Tility**

eBay management services come in two forms: as a desktop application or as a web-based utility. A desktop application works just like any other program on your computer. You will need to download the software to your computer, install it, and configure it to connect to your eBay account. The files, database, and software reside entirely on your computer, which makes it faster than waiting for a web site to load and reload. A web-based utility is a web site through which you manage your listings. These utilities work through your web browser just like any popular e-mail service (GMail, Yahoo!Mail, MSN, etc.). You will not need to download anything and can access your management tools from anywhere. There are benefits and drawbacks to each type of management utility. The best solution for you will depend on your unique needs.

ₕElpful ₕInt

Desktop Application
Pros: Often faster than a web-based solution; easy backup of files and listing database.
Cons: Operating system-dependent; large programs may require a computer upgrade.

Web-Based Utility
Pros: Accessible from anywhere; operating system-independent.
Cons: Can be slow, especially on slow Internet connections; may have browser requirements.

ₜRumbull's ₛTumbles

When Trumbull Mountain first decided on an eBay management utility, they wrongly assessed the importance of being able to access their eBay listings from anywhere. It seemed very important at the expansion's launch that the eBay management job not be tied to one computer in the form of a desktop application. Therefore, they limited their search to only web-based management services. This was a poor decision given their setup, for a few reasons. First, their offices are limited to a dial-up connection. This made the tasks of reloading the utility's web pages, uploading photos, and saving text take hours longer than necessary. Second, the web-based utility they chose did not offer the reporting tools that they wrongly assumed would be included. This left them scratching their heads when it came to end-of-the-month reporting.

They quickly recognized their error and moved their eBay management to a desktop application where the process was much faster. Uploading the prepared listings still took a good amount of time but could be done automatically overnight while the office was closed. The new desktop management software saved Trumbull Mountain hundreds of dollars in employee time.

For proper reporting, Trumbull Mountain learned not to depend on their eBay management tools at all, but rather their existing inventory and retail management program.

eSsential cOmponents

There are a few things that every eBay management service or utility must do. These key components are essential in making your management time efficient and effective. Not all of the eBay management utilities you test will offer all of these services, and therefore you may, for example, end up using one program for listing management and another service for e-mail management. If you do find that you like several features of several pay programs or services, you will likely find that the free tools from eBay will do several of these task admirably. Be sure to explore eBay's free offerings before you conclude that you need to pay several different services for access to several different features.

Customizable Templates

The beautiful design that you have created for your listings should be easily saved into your listing management program for easy duplication for each new listing you create. The trouble of recreating, or cutting and pasting, your template code for each listing you submit will be prohibitive. Make sure that the eBay management program that you select allows you to create your own custom template, and then save it for reuse whenever you need it.

Automatic Relist or Repost

The trick to keeping 10,000 items in your store is to automate the relisting of your items. Once you have created a listing page for an item, it must be possible for you to automate the relisting or reposting of that item. Even if you only have a few hundred items listed in your eBay Store, if 30 of them end in a single night, it could take you several hours to double-check their price, information, photos, duration, and title of each one before relisting it. Asking your eBay management program to keep items that you've already checked for accuracy online will save you hours of work every week.

hElpful hint

There is an important difference between relisting an item and reposting it. Relisting unsold items is a simple matter of telling eBay to make your unsold item available again. This makes you eligible for eBay's relisting discount. Reposting items means that you re-upload all of the item's information and photos again. The new posting is considered an entirely new listing by eBay. There is no discount for entirely reposting unsold items.

Automated E-mails

Communicating with your customers will consume a great deal of your time. You can minimize this amount of time by automating many of the regular e-mails that customers need to receive throughout the purchasing process. These e-mails include invoices, winner notivations, shipping notifications, feedback requests, and more. Most web-based eBay management utilities will offer e-mail automation. Web-based utilities are able to do this more easily because the servers on which they reside have a constant connection to the Internet and can therefore monitor your sales activity. Desktop applications have a harder time doing this because often the computer on which the program resides will be off, or not connected to the Internet. eBay's Selling Manager Pro offers e-mail automation if your preferred listing manager does not.

WYSIWYG HTML Editor

One of the most useful components of any eBay management tool is the WYSIWYG (What You See Is What You Get) HTML editor. For nontechnical folks who don't know and don't want to learn how to code HTML, these WYSIWYG editors can be incredibly helpful in translating your formatting ideas to the web site.

tRial pEriods

Testing dozens of eBay management tools can grow to be outrageously expensive if you pay the monthly fee for each one you test. Luckily many of these utilities offer a trial period during which you can test the full functionality of the utility without committing your-self to pay every month. There are also many free eBay management utilities that will never ask you to cough up any money. These free tools can be quite good for limited usage, but if you're looking for a robust tool to make your business run more smoothly, you won't find any for free.

pAyment pLans

Be aware of how these utilities require you to submit payment. The ideal payment plan is a flat monthly fees with no surprises. However, you will run into more intricate payment plans that will charge you a monthly fee for their basic service and then incrementally throughout the month for any upgrades you use. Also, you will find plans with no monthly rate, but that will charge you a small amount per transaction. These per-transaction fees may seem low, but remember that they are coming at the end of an already long line of per-transaction fees. With so many quality tools on the market, you shouldn't have to surrender more profit per item to your management tools.

Marketing Strategies

muscling your way into any marketplace takes time. It is impossible for any business owner—no matter how savvy—to roll a hot dog cart into a sea of 200 million other hot dog carts and instantly become top dog (or dog-seller). You will need to invest some time establishing your business on eBay, and on eBay's terms. Your feedback rating must be high. Your descriptions and images must be exemplary. Your store must be well-stocked. These factors will serve as your foundation from which to grow. Real growth on eBay will occur when you master the subtleties of eBay's marketplace and selling platform.

You must learn new methods of advertising. Some techniques are specific to eBay, and some are just good e-commerce practices in general. The traditional marketing techniques that you're used to will not be your most effective. Newspaper ads, printed flyers, and radio spots may work well for your retail store, but they are not the best ways to connect with your eBay buyers. It's hard to hear a radio advertisement in Billings when you're at home shopping in Albany.

This chapter will introduce you to some new ways to market your eBay expansion. These techniques aim to capitalize on eBay's established shopping population, and to bring in some new shoppers to the marketplace.

mArketing on eBay

Before you start bringing in customers from outside eBay you should make sure that your eBay operation is ready to receive them. The best, and most basic, marketing you can do for your business on eBay is to present your business and your items well. This means that you should use custom-designed description templates that incorporate your company's logo, colors, and contact information. You should also make sure that your item photography is on a par with the best on eBay. This does not mean you need to spend thousands of dollars on professional product shots, as there are cheap ways to produce great images. (See Chapter 5, Photography, for more.)

You will need to build a solid foundation of great aesthetic design, exhaustive item descriptions, complete and clearly stated policy statements, several running auctions, and a decently stocked store. From this point you can begin to employ the following more advanced techniques for drawing in more traffic.

Auctions as Ads

One of your main goals on eBay is to sell as much as possible through your store. Store listings are less costly than auctions, they last longer, the sales are instant, and the prices are fixed. This means that you do less work for more money.

The problem is that your store items are largely invisible to buyers cruising through eBay's auction stream. eBay's main search function doesn't include your store items, and unless a casual shopper happens to search specifically for items in a store, your items will not be seen.

In order to create traffic in your eBay store, you need to drop hooks into the auction stream. These hooks come in the form of auctions of your most popular items with low starting prices. Now, it is always scary to list an expensive and popular item for a low starting price when you know you could sell it easily in your retail store for full price, but it is a means to an end. And, more often than not, you won't lose money on these auctions.

Here's how the strategy works. You create an auction for an item that has been proven—through research or experience—to draw lots of attention on eBay. This item must be related to your main category of items in order for this strategy to work. Selling iPods to promote your tire warehouse will not produce favorable results for you. On this auction page, in addition to all the usual information about the popular item, place mini-advertisements for your store and for related items in your store. There are many ways to do this, some of which I'll cover below.

Once you've got your auction ad perfected with lots of information, pretty pictures, and links to related store items, begin the auction with a starting price of $0.99 and no reserve price. Schedule it to end during one of eBay's peak traffic times. The goal of this auction is not profitability, but promotion. Sometimes you will lose money on these no-reserve auctions. Think of it as a paid advertisement for your eBay store. With its low starting price, and high popularity, this auction should garner a lot of attention. This auction will drive traffic to your eBay store.

To increase the effectiveness of this strategy, upgrade your auction ad listings to include the use of bolding, highlights, a border, and a gallery photo. If you would really like your item to draw in customers, spend the extra $19.95 and select eBay's Featured Plus! package that promotes your item in the site's "Featured" boxes. Once you've perfected this technique with one auction, begin running several every week, all ending at various times. This can be a great way to hook in buyers that are interested in your products and shuffle them along to your most profitable items. And, as a bonus, if you've selected highly popular items, you will find that often the sale price for these sacrificial items can meet or exceed your desired selling price.

Your ultimate goal with these auctions, as with any auctions, is to create a bidding war between buyers. During a bidding war, the buyer's most important objective becomes winning the item, not getting a great deal. These $0.99 auctions do a great job of getting hordes of shoppers to bid early and emotionally invest themselves in taking the item home. The more bidders you can hook early, the better your chances will be for creating a bidding war, and driving up your final sale price.

These sacrificial item auctions are guaranteed to sell. The first bid of $0.99 secures the sale. Therefore, it can be smart to select the appropriate accessory products from your store to advertise on this item's auction page. Trumbull Mountain puts popular models of used saddles out into the auction stream. On the auction pages for these saddles they have several links to their store, and advertise the girths, leathers, stirrups, and so on that would fit with this particular saddle. The winning bidder has no doubt spent several days checking this auction page repeatedly to watch bidding activity, so these little store item advertisements on Trumbull Mountain's auction page present a great opportunity for them to do some upselling. Quite often this tactic is successful for them.

Your eBay management software should have some tools available to help you insert cross-promotion into your auction pages. eBay's store manager has some tools that help you to cross-promote categories of items within your store. That way, once you've got the customer looking at a store item, the cross-promotion links keep the customer inside your store.

This in-store cross-promotion tool is accessible from within your Manage My Store page. Click the Cross-Promotion link in the left menu. You are able to set the cross-promotion tool to work automatically, or you can designate which categories other categories promote. For example, Trumbull Mountain has elected to promote items from their bridle category to anyone viewing an item in their saddle category. They've also experimented with promoting their saddle category from every other category, since their main goal is to sell saddles. They found, though, that cross-promoting between categories yields the best results.

King of the Hill

When a person shopping on eBay submits a search for a specific search term for a popular item, thousand of search results pop up. The default number of listings displayed on the first page of results is 40. A promotion tactic of many sellers is to schedule 40 auctions for the same item to end within a few minutes of one another. This guarantees that when a user searches for that item during the closing few hours of those auctions, this seller's items will dominate the page. This strategy is known as packing a category.

This is a clever way to siphon traffic into your listings and store. However, some sellers take it too far and will list hundreds of thousands of auctions to end at all times of day for months at a time. This is incredibly expensive to do, and often fraudulent since these sellers don't have a warehouse full of hundreds of thousands of items. But it also guarantees that this seller will dominate sales for that item in that month. You may run into these tactics from other sellers, and it can be extremely frustrating to be on the losing end. Your item will eventually be shown on the first page of search results during their closing minutes, but it very well could be the only item that doesn't belong to the other seller, giving you only a 1 in 40 chance that your item will be selected during the time when it is supposed to be most visible.

There are a couple of ways to combat this tactic, and some things to learn from it. First, many times when you run into sellers who are packing a category, their listings will be lifted from other sellers. Blue Star frequently finds sellers who are simply copying their photos and descriptions and then, if their sale is successful, reselling Blue Star's goods at a huge markup by tacking on exorbitant shipping fees. By lifting listings from other sellers, category packers are able to list tens of thousands of items that they don't own. The sheer number of their listings guarantees sales. If you run into this, you should report the seller immediately to eBay. Reported listings are removed for investigation and will therefore restore some breathing room to your category.

Sometimes you'll find that what appears to be fraudulent category packing is simply just a larger competitor with a bigger inventory. In this case your auction listings will be squeezed off the first page of search results legitimately. The only way to combat this is to fight fire with fire. Increasing the number of listings you post at one time will increase your presence in your category and increase your sales. It is always a good thing to grow within your category. The more items you offer within a specific page of search results, the more likely buyers are to click into your auctions.

If you have a limited inventory to work with, and can't afford to double or triple its size in an attempt to dominate your category for the month, you can try, instead, to own it for a day, a week, even an evening. Try listing all of one type of your eBay auction inventory to end during one of eBay's peak traffic times. For example, Trumbull Mountain could list all their saddle pads to end on Sunday at 9 pm Pacific Standard Time. Instead of spreading their dozens of saddle pads out over a period of a few weeks, they can pack the saddle pad category for that one night by listing them all at once. In this way, they become the evening's main supplier of saddle pads on eBay. The money they take in from that one night of saddle pad selling bliss, they could reinvest into more saddle pads—this time trying to dominate the category for two nights a week. By repeating this process, their sales and profits will grow to a point where they could very well become the largest saddle pad dealer on eBay. After conquering the saddle pad category, they could move on to bridles, bits, stirrups, and so on.

As eBay is an open marketplace, there are no controls in place to help small sellers. Even when the tools, listings, and items are the same for everybody, the largest bird still usually gets the worm. Listing a few items at a time will not always produce the results you desire. Remember, you're operating in a category with thousands of other sellers. Instead of tossing some needles into the haystack, you should shove a bull into the china cabinet. Act big, even if you only have the resources available to do so for one evening a month. By giving yourself the best chance to create sales, you will improve your chances for growth.

sTrategy sNippet

Nowhere are the laws of supply and demand more alive than on eBay. Be careful not to list too many identical items at one time. To do so will remove any sense of urgency a buyer had about buying the item, and your final sale prices will suffer. If you plan on packing the category, list multiple sizes, colors, and styles of items. Not only will this better serve the wide range of tastes among your customers, but it will not be too damaging to the sense of urgency in buyers who are lusting after one specific style of your item.

The keys to making this strategy successful are to select popular items to sell, and to schedule your auctions to end during a time that you know your buyers are on eBay. Listing all your NFL player jerseys to end on Monday nights—eBay's second highest traffic night—just because it is a high traffic night is ignoring the fact that your most likely buyers will be watching Monday Night Football. If you plan on putting all your eggs in one basket, be sure that your customers are standing around the basket waiting to buy.

Store Upgrades

As mentioned in Chapter 6, eBay's Selling Options, eBay offers several levels of store subscriptions. The basic store program is cheap but comes with no built-in promotional deals. The Featured store program will place a text link prominently on the Stores Directory and Stores gateway page. Links are also placed in the "Shop eBay Stores" box of appropriate search results pages. Anchor stores provide quite a bit more built-in promotion. They will display your store's logo as an advertisement at the top of the eBay Stores gateway page and will also display links to your items around the site as the Featured program does.

Taking advantage of the two more expensive store programs can significantly boost traffic to your store, particularly the Anchor level of subscription. However, because the Anchor level is so expensive—nearly $500 per month—you will need to seriously examine the cost-benefit of making this switch.

mArketing to the bEyond

eBay is huge and growing every day, but it is still merely a dot on the map of the Internet's larger shopping universe. Setting up shop on eBay allows you to tap into eBay's steady stream of traffic, but it also provides you with the tools necessary to make your items easily accessible to every Internet buyer. Promoting your eBay operation on other Internet sites and in the real world can increase your eBay traffic by orders of magnitude. Some methods of off-eBay advertising can prove to be expensive, some are quick and free, and some eBay will even pay you to do.

Following are the most effective methods for off-eBay advertising. You should begin with these techniques as soon as you get your on-eBay operation and promotions working like a well-oiled machine. When it feels like you can't grow anymore (or fast enough) using established on-eBay marketing techniques, it is these strategies that will elevate your eBay operation to the next level.

Your Own Web Site

The first place you should set up some off-eBay marketing is on your own web site. The visitors to your web site are no doubt interested in the items you have to offer. And whether you offer your own e-commerce store or not, your web site's visitors will be interested to know that you have put together an eBay operation. They'll hunt for bargains in your auctions and new items in your store, and check your various informational pages. Your current customers will initially have the most interest in your new eBay operation. Make it easy for them to find it.

There are several ways to promote your eBay sales from your web site. You could place a simple link or graphic banner advertising your eBay Store. This would send a lot of traffic from your web site to your eBay items. And if you didn't offer online shopping previously, this is a great way to serve the large portion of your web site's traffic that would like to buy from you instantly.

A better way to promote your eBay items from your web site is to sign up for eBay's Affiliate Program and to use the tools that it provides. eBay's Affiliate Program is intended to reward individuals and businesses who have sent interested shoppers to eBay. The program is open to everyone, whether an eBay member or not. All affiliate members earn up to 65% commission on eBay revenue and up to a $22 commission for new active user referrals. By signing up for this free program you can earn a commission back on your own sales just for promoting your own items. It's eBay's way of thanking you for using their selling platform.

The affiliate program provides many useful tools to help you create affiliate links to eBay. Using these tools, affiliate members can create many different types of commissioned links to any eBay item or page. eBay sellers, naturally, usually promote only their own items.

The most useful tool is what eBay calls the Editor Kit. Using this web-based tool, you can create banner advertisements that show photos, prices, and ending times for your active items on eBay. You can specify banner template, color, and shape to suit your tastes. But the real power of this tool is that it allows you to specify which items to present based on keyword, price range, purchasing options available, and seller. Therefore you can build banners that promote only your items, and only your most profitable items at that.

The Editor Kit produces what it calls a code "sniplet"—probably because "snippet" is copyrighted somewhere—that you then cut and paste into your web site's HTML code. And that's it. The banner will update the products it displays based on the criteria you've specified and you will earn commission on every sale. (See examples on next page.)

Other tools the affiliate program offers are: a custom banners and buttons tool to help you create links to specific pages on eBay; a Product Kit that works much like the Editor Kit though with more aesthetic customization options; a flexible destination tool that allows you to create a text link to any eBay page; a keyword and UPC code linking tool; a full dynamic landing page for your web site; and an RSS feed generator that can help you to place RSS feeds on your web site that list any combination of products from your auctions or store.

Feeds

Feeds can be put to good use for you in a number of ways. The first example, outlined above, will provide the visitors to your web site the opportunity to subscribe their feed readers to a constantly and automatically updated list of all your items on eBay. Another way to use your feed is, instead of sending the list of your items down to your customers, you can send it up to shopping web sites that use feeds such as yours to build product databases.

> ### hElpful hInt
> A "feed" can be thought of as the internet's cousin of the news ticker. A feed is a constant refreshing flow of information—created automatically by web sites—to which visitors can subscribe.

right now on eBay

Thorowgood Airoform Synthetic Girth 46" Black New
$39.95   15d 23h 40m

Thorowgood Airoform Synthetic Girth 54 Black NEW
$39.95   15d 23h 45m

View all 10 items on eBay   disclaimer

right now on eBay

Looney Tunes Kids Saddle Pad, Sylvester, Red NEW
$39.95   1d 21h 33m

LOONEY TUNES SADDLE PAD BUGS BUNNY BLUE NEW
$39.95   1d 21h 42m

Baines Capriole Dressage Saddle 18 Wide Demo Used
$1,400.00   2d 01h 36m

View all   disclaimer

Two of the promotional boxes that you can create with the Editor Kit and place on your company's web site

Comparison shopping sites and search engines, such as Google, Froogle, Shopping.com, PriceGrabber, and others, use product data feeds to build their search results. By registering your feed with these types of services, you can easily publish your entire eBay inventory instantly to millions of new Internet users.

If you conduct a search on Froogle, for example, you will be presented with item photos, descriptions, price, and seller information for thousands of items. When a user clicks on any listing they are taken directly to the item page on the seller's web site—in your case to your eBay listing page.

You have many possible feeds from which to choose. You can publish a feed of all your items on eBay, of just the items in your store, or of items that fit into a specific keyword search. I suggest using the feed of all your items unless you are publishing it to a specific service where some of your items will not fit.

hElpful hInt

Here's a list to get you started. These are popular comparison shopping sites to which you can submit your eBay Store's data feed.

BizRate (www.bizrate.com)

Calibex (www.calibex.com)

C|Net Shopper (http://shopper.cnet.com)

DealTime (www.dealtime.com)

DigitalSaver (www.digitalsaver.com)

EveryPrice (www.everyprice.com)

Froogle (www.froogle.com)

MonsterMarketplace (www.monstermarketplace.com)

MySimon (www.mysimon.com)

NexTag (www.nextag.com)

PriceFish (www.pricefish.com)

PriceGrabber (www.pricegrabber.com)

PriceHead (www.pricehead.com)

PriceScan (www.pricescan.com)

ShopCartUSA (www.shopcartusa.com)

Shopping.com (www.shopping.com)

Shopzilla (www.shopzilla.com)

Yahoo! Shopping (www.shopping.yahoo.com)

Some of these services will require periodic maintenance of your feeds. Unfortunately, not every service allows for one-time publishing with automatic updates. Some require that you resubmit your feed link every time it updates. If your store inventory is relatively stable and only changes every 30 days or so, then this may not be too much of an inconvenience. However, if you find that your items change every day, this could become bothersome. Luckily, though, you will find that this will only be a problem with the smaller shopping services. Large services, such as Froogle, which is operated by the Google Base program, often offer utilities to make the task of updating easier. Google Base offers the Google Base Store Connector program for Windows PCs at **http://base.google.com/base/storeconnector**.

Find all the shopping and search engine feed submission utilities that you can. It never hurts to expose your items to as wide an audience as possible. For a few hours of extra work, and no financial investment, you can increase the visibility of your items by several millions of online shoppers.

E-mail Marketing

Your eBay Store subscription is enabled with an e-mail marketing utility. This tool can be extremely handy for collecting the contact information for willing recipients of your promotional e-mails about your eBay sales. However, your e-mail marketing should not be limited to this tool. Any retail business that does business online should conduct some level of opt-in e-mail marketing. Designing and sending an e-mail newsletter to thousands of subscribed customers is an extremely fast, cheap, and effective method of promotion, especially if you use eBay's newsletter service, which handles all the computer resource, security, and failed address issues for you. eBay's newsletter tool also allows you to add customized promotional boxes to your e-mail, such as your featured items, featured categories, and best sellers.

Unfortunately, eBay does not allow you to add e-mail addresses to your existing eBay newsletter subscriber list, nor does it let you view or export the e-mail addresses on your subscriber list. Therefore, if you already have an e-mail database of your customers, there's no way to combine the two lists, which would be ideal.

If you don't already have an e-mail mailing list set up on your own web site, I suggest you put one up immediately. By placing a simple box in the corner of your web site, you can collect e-mail addresses from interested customers.

In your e-mail newsletters you should always promote your eBay Store. Whether you place text links, simple photo links, or complicated item boxes, you should always provide a direct link from your e-mails to your items. You're asking too much from your busy customer if they need to open a web browser, type in an address, surf to your eBay Store, and then find the items you've placed on sale.

There is a thin line you must carefully walk between e-mail marketing and spam. E-mail marketers send solicited e-mails to willing recipients who can unsubscribe from the newsletter at any time. Spammers send unsolicited e-mail that can't be opted out of. Willing recipients can become unwilling recipients very quickly if you begin to send too many e-mails—one per week is generally regarded as the safe frequency limit. Be careful not to wear out your welcome.

Print

There is a curious phenomenon taking place within the retail business community. Established retail businesses sometimes hide their eBay operations from their current customers. This behavior baffles me. Your expansion to eBay should be treated just like any other new sales channel. If you opened another retail store location, would you not do everything you could to promote it? Sometimes sellers treat their eBay operations as an afterthought, or as the shameful side of the business.

If you have built and conduct your eBay operation in a professional manner, there is no reason to hide it from your real-world customers. People have fun shopping on eBay and are most likely interested to hear about the expansions of a business they frequent. The garage-sale connotation that eBay once held, and that scared sellers away, is largely extinct. You should feel proud to display the address to your eBay Store on all your printed promotional materials such as business cards, letterhead, calendars, promotional flyers, and print advertising.

I don't suggest launching a large real-world advertising campaign devoted solely to your eBay expansion, only due to the fact that online marketing is so much more cost-effective when promoting a web site. Shoppers can't "click" a link they read in their newspaper, and it's not often that an ad is so compelling that a person will spend the time to get up off the couch, move to the computer, type in the web address, and find out what it is you have to sell. It's much easier to motivate online shoppers to simply "Click Here!"

I do encourage you, however, to include your eBay Store web address in any print, radio, and television advertising you were planning on doing anyway. It is a viable sales channel and one that many buyers prefer.

Paid Online Advertising

If you've been operating your own independent e-commerce site you're probably familiar with paid online advertising programs such as Google's AdWords and Yahoo! Search Marketing (formerly Overture). If you are not using any of these services to promote your web site, this is a good opportunity to get started. Making use of these services can increase the traffic to your web site exponentially overnight. You should employ their services for both your business web site, and your eBay Store.

Paid online advertising programs simply sell advertising space to businesses. The largest such program is Google's AdWords program. Users of this program construct brief advertisements. These ads are most often text, but image and video ads are available as well. Search Google for "wrenches" and you will see the brief textual ads from businesses that have indicated that their ad would appeal to anybody searching for "wrenches." All these ads are keyword-targeted so that Google can display relevant ads to (hopefully) interested shoppers.

In return for displaying ads alongside Google search results, advertisers pay a predetermined fee each time a Google user clicks on their ad. This payment method is referred to as cost-per-click (CPC). The attractive thing about CPC advertising is that you, as an advertiser, only pay for successful conversions. Your advertisement may be shown 200,000 times per day, but if it is only clicked twice, you only pay for two clicks.

The price you pay per click is determined by a bidding system. You submit a bid for the amount you're willing to pay per conversion. If other advertisers are willing to pay more, their ads will be shown more often, and higher up on the page. If you are willing to pay the most, your ad will be shown at the very top of the sponsor section the most frequently. This can be a very effective, and very expensive, service. Google asks that you specify a daily budget for it to honor. If you specify that you can spend only $10 per day, and you're paying $0.50 per click, you ad will be shown for as long as it takes to receive 20 clicks. This could mean your ad stops showing at 8:30 am, or it could run all day. This depends on the effectiveness of your ad. Most ads achieve a 1% click-to-display rate. An ad that achieves 3% or higher is performing well.

Another method of paying for online ads is called cost-per-thousand (CPM). Advertisers using a CPM campaign pay the agreed upon amount for every 1,000 ads shown. This method of payment does not bother with click-through rates at all. This is a more traditional method of paying for advertising, and it is simply based on the number of times an ad is displayed.

I suggest you begin your online advertising with Google's AdWords program. It is the largest, and most well-known, advertising service on the Internet. Not only does Google command over 90% of the Internet's search engine traffic, but its associated advertiser network of independent web site publishers, through the Adsense program, is far and away the Internet's largest. Your ads will be displayed not only on Google's main search results, but on thousands of other web sites across the Internet—wherever your ad would be most relevant. For maximum exposure for your advertisements, Google is a safe first choice.

You should run two main campaigns: one for your business web site, and one for your eBay Store. Google provides many tips and full-length guides on how to select proper keywords to target, and how then to construct effective online advertising. The task may seem

hElpful hInt

When you create your AdWords ad, you will be asked to supply a web address that users won't see, but to which Google will redirect them. You will also be asked to supply an address that Google will display to its users. For example, you can insert the link http://stores.ebay.com/My-Widget-Store as the redirect address, and the more attractive www.mywidgetstore.com/ebay address as the displayed address.

Here are two tips on how to make the best use of this feature.

1. Make sure that whatever address you insert as the display address is an actual address that will send users to the supplied redirect address if manually typed into the user's web browser.

2. Use an eBay Affiliate link as your redirect address. By supplying a link that you've created through eBay's Affiliate tools, you will earn a commission when shoppers that are sent to you from Google make a purchase anywhere on eBay—which will hopefully be from you.

rather simple, but I assure you there is a delicate science behind buyer psychology—a science that Google has nearly perfected and can no doubt make less esoteric. Visit **https://adwords.google.com/select/library/index.html** for some tips on creating effective ads.

Businesses that do not operate their own e-commerce site may want to focus more attention and money toward their eBay Store advertising campaign. People who search on Google using product brand names are usually looking to make or research a purchase online. By sending them to your eBay Store, that shopper will have the option to make a purchase immediately, whereas they may not have that option from your business's web site.

Delivering the Goods

Shipping is an essential piece of any business selling on eBay. There are 194 million new items posted to eBay every month, and nearly every one of them is shipped to the buyer after the sale. Even large items such as motorcycles, pool tables, and dishwashers are packed into freight containers and sent around the world to anxiously awaiting eBay bidders and buyers. This, of course, has been a huge boon to the shipping industry, which is why you'll see that nearly every major carrier now advertises directly to eBay sellers.

With the help of eBay, local retail businesses are expanding to serve global markets. And each small retail business needs reliable, high-quality shipping services. Luckily, the biggest shipping services, such as UPS, FedEx, DHL, and others, are making their services more accessible to small businesses and individuals. You'll now see a FedEx everywhere there used to be a Kinkos, and a UPS where there was a Mailboxes Etc. Unlike 10 years ago, you can now find several worldwide shipping services in every small town across the country.

This is wonderful news for eBay sellers, as an efficient global shipping system is a necessity once you begin selling on eBay. Whether you ship 10 items a day or 10 thousand, the time you spend now designing an intelligent shipping process will save you time and money later.

Your shipping speed and accuracy will have a direct effect on your eBay feedback rating. The most common complaints that eBay sellers receive is for sending buyers the wrong item, or the right item too slowly.

For businesses that are already accustomed to shipping many items every day, the process of expanding to eBay will be a natural extension to the existing business, though for a business with retail locations that rarely ships an item to a customer, setting up a proper shipping system will be one of the largest obstacles to getting started. A shipping department will require careful layout, shipping and packing materials, integration into the business's inventory software, and, of course, plenty of physical space.

Many businesses, when they make the leap to eBay, begin packing and shipping in the limited space they have available to them. Unfortunately, this is often a necessity due to budget or building constraints. If the number of daily sales is small enough, businesses can operate under space constraints without too much trouble or error. However, if your goal with eBay goes beyond selling a few items every day for extra revenue, you will need to make arrangements to move your shipping department out of the back hall and into its own dedicated space.

This chapter will help you to define your shipping requirements, lay out a basic shipping department, and select a carrier based on the needs of your business. The first task in setting up a shipping system is to define your system's goals.

gOals

The goals of your shipping system are largely dictated by the expectations of your eBay buyers. The system you build should meet the needs of your business, in terms of efficiency and operating costs, but it also must meet the needs of your customers. For example, many eBay businesses are run by only one or two people. Therefore, in order to fit all the work that needs doing into one week, they have elected to condense all their shipping duties to one day a week. While this works well for the business by freeing up the rest of the week for the other necessary tasks, it does not serve their customers well. You may need to sacrifice some of your own business comforts to better serve the needs of your customers.

Speed

One of the first goals of your shipping department should be speed. The time between the moment an item sells on eBay and the moment it is carried away by the shipping carrier should be as brief as possible. At the time of actual purchase, many auction winners will have been already waiting anxiously for a week or longer just to purchase the item—you should do everything you can to make sure they don't have to wait another week to receive it. Here are a few ways to maximize shipping speed.

Prompt Packing. The shipping process should begin as early as possible after payment is received for a sale. How this process is started will vary with the size of the business. Large businesses should have an instant, automated notification system in place and a shipping queue for sales that come in during off-business hours. Ideally, this would be handled by the company's inventory management software. The shipping department should receive the item's inventory code, shipping address, and method of shipping either the first thing in the morning or within minutes of the item's sale if it comes in during the day.

In smaller businesses the shipping process is usually started by e-mail, instant message, or telephone. In some cases, the eBay sales manager will simply get up from his desk and pack the item himself. In each case, the item should be ready to ship on the same, or next, business day.

Layout. The physical layout of your shipping area will be a large factor in determining the efficiency of your shipping process. A cluttered, cramped space will lead to errors and damaged goods. You should have plenty of room for a large packing table, all your packing materials, a computer, and a stack of "ready-to-go" items.

In many cases a large amount of space is a luxury small businesses just don't have. If this is true in your business, try to find clever ways to maximize the space that is available to you. For example, when you can't expand horizontally, expand vertically. A well-built shelving system can make great use of the space above your packing table. Lightweight materials such as packing peanuts, the foam roll, air bags, and small boxes can be stored above the packer's head. Underneath the packing table, consider using a rolling supply cart. It could serve as regular shelving for you by holding the more common packing materials such as packing tape and mailing labels, but it could also be rolled out to provide you with more table space when necessary.

If your business has, or can acquire, plenty of room for a shipping department, you'll have a much easier time building an efficient system. For more about ideal shipping layouts, see the Set-Up section later in this chapter.

Pick-up/Drop-off. You should be shipping items every business day. Your customers will appreciate it, and your feedback rating will be better off because of it. There are two methods for shipping every day: pick-up or drop-off.

Most of the major carriers will happily come to your location every business day for a monthly fee. UPS visits Trumbull Mountain Tack Shop every day at three o'clock to pick up their awaiting saddle shipments. FedEx has a similar service, and even the USPS will pick up any number of packages from you for a $13.25 per pick-up fee—which is so expensive that it isn't feasible for every day pickups, but for the odd package traveling internationally, this service could be handy. Call your preferred carrier to request a recurring pick-up schedule.

Your other option, of course, is to drop off your shipments at your carrier yourself. This may seem like the less expensive alternative, but when you consider fuel costs and the time you or your employee spends standing in line, this option can be quite pricey. If you choose to drop off shipments every day, you will need a vehicle capable of transporting your packages in one load—making multiple trips every day to UPS or the Post Office is a bad solution.

Accuracy

Speed is nothing without accuracy. The quickest way to sink your feedback rating is to mix up shipments. Remember, buyers have been anxiously waiting for their items to arrive—sometimes for as long as 10 days. The disappointment that they feel when their exciting new Quad-Core CPU turns out to be a box of boring USB cables will send most buyers straight to eBay to strike back with negative feedback. There are some measures you can take to ensure that mistakes are few and far between.

Inventory Code. Every item in your inventory should have a unique identifying code. In all likelihood, if you use inventory management software, this code is automatically generated and assigned. It is important that this code specifies a unique item, as many businesses will have similar types of items that vary only by traits that may not be easily identifiable upon a quick glance.

For example, Trumbull Mountain Tack Shop stocks hundreds of saddles in a relatively small space. They carry many lines of saddle styles, with many sizes in each style. Without close inspection, a 17.5" black all-purpose Wintec saddle is not easily distinguishable from the 18" black all-purpose Wintec saddle. Without an identifying code to guide the person doing the shipping, it would very easy to grab and ship the wrong saddle. The identifying code speeds up the inventory-picking process by reducing it to a matter of matching numbers, not seeking out specifics on an item's tags.

Packing Slips. In with each item that ships, you should include a packing slip that contains the following information:

- item name
- item's eBay photo
- item inventory code
- item description
- eBay item number
- selling price
- shipping address
- return address
- company contact information
- up-sell information

This packing slips serves three purposes. First, it helps the person doing the shipping quickly make sure that the item sold is the item in the box. The shipper will be able to glance quickly at the inventory code and item photo on the packing slip and double-check that no mistake has been made.

Second, the packing slip gives customers all pertinent information regarding the sale. If a customer needed to contact your company for any reason regarding the sale, he or she would be able to provide all the information necessary for you to look up the sale in your records.

Finally, the packing slip provides a great opportunity to advertise your other products to people you know to be already interested. This can be a low-cost, yet highly effective way to advertise holiday sales, close-out items, or even complimentary accessory items for the item you've just shipped.

Software. There are hundreds of inventory management programs available to help you keep track of, and streamline, your shipping process. If you are currently using software to track your inventory, I suggest using the program with which you're comfortable. This is one aspect of expansion to eBay where it isn't necessary to make changes to your system.

However, if you are currently not using software to manage your inventory, I strongly suggest that you select software that includes shipping management. It will require an investment of time and money to get started, but it will be well worth it in the long run. Please see Chapter 4 for more about inventory management.

The two major carriers that most eBay sellers use—UPS and FedEx—both provide shipping management software. This software is designed to make the process of printing labels, submitting payment, and tracking shipments easier for sellers. To learn more about each program, visit the links below.

UPS WorldShip: www.ups.com/orderworldship
FedEx Ship Manager: www.fedex.com/us/solutions/software/

In order to use either of these programs, you will need to register for an account with the respective company. Do extensive research into each company before you commit to using just one. The services from FedEx and UPS vary greatly in terms of ability and price. Conduct several shipment quotes for each type of item you expect to normally ship. Compare prices, speed, and pick-up options.

yOur sHipping sEetup

When designing your shipping department it is important to consider "item flow." Items should travel in succession from inventory, to packing, to the trucks. This succession should be logically and physically straightforward.

Blue Star Computers moved from location to location during the growth of their company. They have seen a lot of different shipping configurations in their time and therefore understand the importance of setting up your system for success. When they made their most recent move to their Holliston location, one of the most important decision factors in selecting a space was the available area for their shipping department. They chose a building that provided enough space for them to set up an ideal situation given their size and inventory control system. They have perfected "flow." This physical and logical flow allows employees to come and go in and out of the system during the course of a day. The system inherently tracks inventory so that one person doesn't need to. Any person will know, upon stepping into the system, which items need to be sent where. This creates a system where communication isn't necessary for the system to run smoothly.

At the rear of their building they have two very large loading docks, each with its own garage-style warehouse door. They decided to receive packages through one door, and send them out through the other. This simple decision forms the basis of their entire inventory and shipping processes.

A wall separates the two loading bays. Trucks drop off their incoming inventory on one side of the wall and pick up their shipments on the other. Within the warehouse, the items travel through a series of steps. See Chapter 4 for more about inventory control. Blue Star has set up their shipping department so that items can travel from their inventory shelves straight out the shipping door. There is no backtracking or juggling involved.

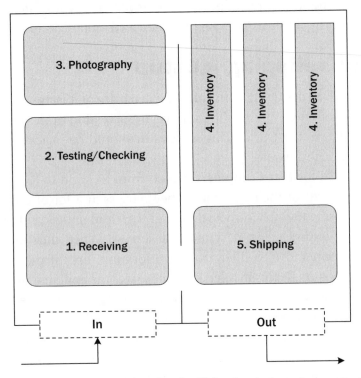

A sample layout similar to Blue Star's. This simple layout, on any scale, will work well for your business.

If you don't have the luxury of a large warehouse with two loading docks, you can still make use of this efficient layout. Within the space you have available to you, create a sequential system of steps through which your items will travel. Try to devote a physical space to each step, and mark it, if necessary, with a sign. This could be as basic as different parts of your packing table, or it could be different corners of the room. Apply the intentions of the layout shown in the figure to whatever space you have available.

One of the best ways to speed up your shipping department is by using powerful inventory control software. This software should be able to manage every step of your shipping process. One of the places where this can help you most is in the area of item picking. For example, when a sale is logged into a quality inventory control program, it is added to a list of "ready-to-ship" items. Employees in the shipping department can print out this list of items, which contains inventory numbers, warehouse location, and quantities. The list is ordered, by the software, in such a way that the employee in charge of picking these items off the warehouse shelves can proceed successively up and down the aisles. Because the inventory software created the warehouse's shelving map, it knows exactly where each item is located and routes the employees picking out items in the most efficient route. This can prevent hours of wasted employee time searching through a roughshod shelving system.

When selecting inventory control software, it should do more than track the number of items you have in stock. Have your shipping department in mind when you are shopping for software.

mAterials

Your shipping materials will depend on the items you're shipping and the carrier you're using. Some carriers have strict package size and shape restrictions (like the USPS), while others will deliver nearly anything you are able to hand over (like DHL).

If you're packing fragile items, such as glassware, computer components, or macaroni figurines, you will need to use appropriate packing materials. Wadded newspaper and paper-towel wrap is not professional and your buyers will fault you for it.

There are many great places to research your packing material options. And there are many great space-saving alternatives to gigantic bags of packing peanuts and rolls of foam wrap. A good place to start your research is on ULINE's web site. ULINE is one of the largest packing material suppliers in the world. Their catalog is filled with materials and packing tools that most people never realized existed. Before you begin laying out your shipping department, order one of their free catalogs and browse through what they have to offer. You may end up finding that one of their tools will save you thousands of dollars per year, but that it may require some dedicated floor space.

There are some tools and materials you will need regardless of your items and available space. I've included a list of these below, with some tips on where to find them.

Postage Scale. Every carrier will require that you specify an item's weight. Therefore it is essential that you have a reliable scale—and one that is large enough to weigh your heaviest items. eBay abounds with new and used postage scales of varying quality. If you want to make sure that you're getting a quality scale, I suggest you buy new. Pitney Bowes is one of the largest postage scale manufacturers around. They have always been known to produce top-of-the-line products. If you aren't looking for top-of-the-line, cruising through your local Staples, OfficeMax, or Office Depot will present you with a few options.

Boxes. Boxes can be troublesome, as they are large, unwieldy, and come in every size known to man. ULINE has a catalog full of every sort of box you could ever need. If you're using USPS exclusively, you can make use of their promotional free eBay-branded boxes. These are boxes from the USPS with the eBay logo that they will ship to you at no cost in any quantity. The catch is, of course, that these boxes can only be used to send packages through the USPS. To order your free boxes, visit **http://ebay-supplies.usps.com**. UPS offers a similar free box program, though it is limited to their WorldWide Express service. To find out more go to: **www.ups.com/content/us/en/resources/prepare/supplies/boxes.html**.

Tape. You'll need several tape guns and stacks and stacks of rolls and rolls of clear packing tape. This is an item of which you'll need a lot and, because quality isn't much of an issue with tape as long as it's sticky, you can feel pretty safe buying it in bulk at discount prices. eBay is a great place to search for bulk tape. Go to **http://business.ebay.com** and search for "packing tape." You'll find that you can buy cases of 36 rolls for Buy It Now prices around $10. That's a deal you'll never find locally.

Packing Peanuts. I advise against the use of packing peanuts for a number of reasons: they are hard to store, they are messy, their use requires extra protection of the item from peanut dust, and they are environmentally irresponsible. In lieu of using packing peanuts, I recommend using sealed-air cushioning packing bags. These bags are not inflated when you buy them; they arrive on a small roll that can be stored easily. When it comes time to pack an item, you simply feed the bag roll through the inflator, and tear off as many inflated bags as you need to keep the item secure in its box. Buying the inflator will require an initial investment of a few hundred dollars, but this will save you time, money, and frustration in the long run.

sOftware

It is important that you make use of shipping management software. This software will make the tasks of printing labels, paying for service, and tracking shipments much easier on you and your employees. The best software to use will likely come from the carrier service you choose to employ. UPS provides a wonderful program called WorldShip. FedEx provides a similar manager called Ship Manager. Both of these programs will maintain a shipping address book, calculate shipping costs, collect payment, print labels, alert the carrier of shipment creation, schedule pickups, and provide tracking information.

If you choose not to use these two programs, or use a carrier that doesn't provide such software, you can make use of eBay and PayPal's shipping integration tools. Both UPS and the USPS have set up "Zones" on eBay. The USPS Shipping Zone, at **http://pages.ebay.com/usps/home.html**, enables you to manage your shipments from sale to packaging to shipping to tracking. You can print a USPS shipping label from any printer, tape it to your package, and drop it in the mail. UPS has a similar setup in their eBay "Zone" at **http://pages.ebay.com/ups/home.html**.

The usefulness of a quality shipping management utility cannot be understated. When all your sales and eBay reputation depend on quick, reliable delivery of your products to your customers, the ability to manage and track your

hElpful hInt

Trumbull Mountain has been using UPS shipping for years. Every day at 4:00 the UPS truck rumbles down the dirt road between the horse paddocks to pick up the outgoing saddles. The company is thrilled with the service UPS provides, from the WorldShip software to the daily pickups.

sale along every step of its journey is invaluable. You will run into scam artists who claim a package was never received, and if you have no tracking system in place, you're left without recourse. PayPal only accepts verified tracking information from a third party as proof of delivery. Cover yourself by using a shipping management utility for every package you send out the door.

iNternational sHipping

Shipping internationally opens up your items to gigantic markets with gigantic sales potential. It also opens up a new world of troubles. In the case of shipping, sending packages across international borders can eat up your time and your customer's money.

Most eBay sellers elect to use the USPS for all international shipping. The rates are lower, and the forms are fewer. UPS, FedEx, DHL, and all the other big private carriers each have particular international shipping regulations in place. You may need to send a package into a country where these companies don't operate. Therefore they will need to pass off the shipment to an approved local carrier. In order for these major carriers to release responsibility for your packages, they require you to sign countless release forms in addition to all the usual customs and border fees forms. Selecting to use one of these major carriers can easily double the cost and double the amount of time required. For these reasons, shipping internationally is most often done through the USPS.

Shipping internationally through the USPS is no simple matter either. It involves the usual customs forms, border fees, and standing in line at your local post office. Instead of handing off your packages to the FedEx or UPS pick-up truck, you will need to drop off the international shipments yourself. The USPS does offer package pickup service, but it carries a weighty fee and therefore only makes sense for your most profitable sales.

If you do decide to ship internationally, always be on the lookout for improved services from various companies. All the major carriers are working with government officials and foreign shipping companies to make the transport of packages across borders less cumbersome. Some of these improved international services are beginning to come to market already.

Pitney Bowes, the well-known shipping products manufacturer, has branched its offerings into shipping services. They have launched a service called ClearPath, which aims to make the abominable task of shipping overseas more manageable for small businesses. Essentially, they take care of all the paperwork and package handling for you. The service is so simple for business owners to use that I have to assume that Pitney Bowes is populated entirely by logistics geniuses. You ship your packages to their domestic location as you would normally ship any domestic package, and they take care of all the bother involved with sending it overseas. You receive a tracking number, package routing details, and delivery confirmation.

ClearPath is in its growing stages and currently only serves Canadian buyers, though the company tells me that service to additional countries will be available soon. ClearPath is especially valuable to eBay sellers because, when it expands to other countries, it will have torn down one of the largest obstacles to reaching the huge international markets. For more about the ClearPath Cross Border Service from Pitney Bowes, visit **www.pbclearpath.com**.

Whether you are building a shipping department from scratch or refining an already well-managed process, you should find some of the tools and tips above helpful. Shipping is one of the easiest areas of your business where you can impress your customers and get a step on your competition. Be on the lookout for new systems and services that may make your job easier. Check the eBay Solutions directory's shipping category occasionally for ways to improve your service. Your competition will.

eChapter twelve

Customer Care

In many ways, taking care of customers online is exactly the same as taking care of customers in your store. Good service requires that you be professional, friendly, and knowledgeable about your products and policies. In both instances, customers expect the items on display to be well-priced, well-presented, and available for purchase. If your existing business is doing well enough that you're seeking to expand, I can reasonably assume that you've figured out how to serve your customers well. The goal of this chapter is not to drag you through a refresher course in customer service, but rather to point out some places where many competent sellers unintentionally fail at customer service on eBay. Being aware of these pitfalls should help you avoid making the same mistakes.

While there are many common aspects of providing quality customer service between eBay and your store, selling on eBay often requires a few extra steps to ensure customer satisfaction. The well-worn tricks of smiling, chatting about the weather, and handing their kid a lollipop just won't translate to your eBay audience. Thankfully, there are some easy ways you can provide the same level of "above-and-beyond" customer service throughout your customers' eBay buying experience. This chapter highlights some useful tools and tricks you can employ to help you find the fastest route to that Red Shooting Star of your PowerSellin' dreams.

▌lstings

Your customer's experience with your business begins, most often, with one of your listing pages. This is one reason why I stress to all sellers the importance of attractive listing design. Your item's description may be stellar, your price may be unbeatable, and your shipping may be the fastest on eBay, but all of this matters very little if upon arrival to your listing page your customer is smacked in the face with an unprofessional impression of your business. Often, buyers will not stick around to read your policies and description if you provide them with an instantly unfavorable impression of your business. They may also question your low prices.

Just as bad (or no) design will hurt you, great design will help. Striking your customers with an instantly favorable impression of your business makes them more receptive to the information you present, and more forgiving toward any mistakes they find. In the minds of your buyers professional design equates to a professional business. In the world of eBay, buyers often have little on which to gauge a company's trustworthiness. (Feedback stars can't tell the whole story.) Therefore, buyers will scrutinize every detail of your listings for any indications that would help them form an overall impression of your operation. With that in mind, there are a few details—beyond design—which you can add to your listings that will tip the scales in your favor every time.

Description

The description of your items in every listing should be exhaustive and accurate. In many cases your seller may know more about the item you're selling than you do and will catch any mistakes or misprints you publish. Expert collectors of every type scour eBay every day looking for deals. Be sure to double-check your listings for any errors, and confirm any information of which you're unsure.

If you've been shopping on eBay a fair amount, you will no doubt have run into listing descriptions that are by all accounts complete, but incredibly difficult to read. Sometimes sellers overuse font sizes, colors, alignments, and anything else they learned in HTML 101. This creates a listing page that is hard on the eyes and unpleasant to read through. These sellers may have the most beautifully designed listing template on eBay, but it doesn't mean much if the information on it looks like the work of a Crayola-crazed second-grader.

On the opposite end of the spectrum, some sellers use too little formatting in their description text. These descriptions appear as large blocks of tightly-spaced text. They, too, are hard on the eyes and difficult to read through.

Your description text should not lean to either extreme. Rather, it should balance safely in the center where textual formatting does exist, but only in places where it makes the presented information more accessible to excited eyes. As a general rule, the formatting techniques you use to draw attention to selections of information should never add to the clutter on the page. Here are some good formatting techniques to use:

- **Bullet Lists.** Bullet lists are a good way to make item specifics easy to read and quick to glance over.
- **Bold.** Bolding of important points will help your readers skip over all the usual filler words that their minds fill in anyway such as "the," "and," "with," and so on.
- **Indentation.** Indenting will help separate out important bits of description in a subtle, nondisruptive manner.

And some to avoid:

- **Underline.** Underlining a word fills in a space between lines of text that is important to keep open for visual clarity. Unless you are able to provide extra white space beneath the underlined text—as in the case of headers—you should avoid using underlines.
- **Arrows.** Using textual or graphical arrows can be too visually forceful. They impose urgency upon a piece of information that may not particularly appeal to your reader. This false urgency is distracting and annoying.
- **Colors.** As a general rule, changing the colors of text within

your description is a bad idea. The human eye recognizes color before shape, size, distance, or any other visual factors. This can be extremely distracting for readers whose eyes are inadvertently being pulled away from what they're reading to the bright red text in the sidebars. If you choose to use colors in your text, make the changes subtle—a few shade variations of a common color can work well.

■ **Symbols.** Using textual symbols as eye-catchers, such as in "L@@K!" or "!!!!!!!!!!!! or ———->", wastes space, is visually forceful, and can be interpreted as unprofessional.

Aside from the visual construction of your descriptions, their content needs to be carefully thought out as well. I've covered the best information to include when describing items in Chapter 6, eBay's Selling Options, so I won't explain that again here. But in addition to the proper item description, you should include additional general information for your customers on every listing.

Underneath each product description you should devote some space on your listing page to describing your payment policies, your shipping policies, your returns policy, and your checkout process. Providing all this information on every listing page will save you a lot of time in answering questions from uninformed shoppers. It will also save your customers time and frustration by informing them of all your policies before they commit to a purchase.

hElpful pAges

As mentioned earlier, your eBay Store manager allows you to create custom pages on which you can place any sort of information you would like. These pages are sometimes used as additional "About Me" pages, or photo galleries of the shop owner's pets. While these uses can be helpful in promoting a personal familiarity with your customers, I think there is a better use for these pages.

Use these pages to restate your policies just as they have been stated on your listing pages. Shoppers who are browsing your store will not think to click on an item to view your store policies. It is counterintuitive. By restating your policies on a custom page, your store will have a direct link for shoppers to a policies page where they will be easily found.

You should also create some custom pages that will be helpful to shoppers for your specific products. You know your customers best. And therefore you know what a customer is most likely to ask. Create pages that address these popular questions.

Trumbull Mountain goes to great lengths to ensure that every saddle they sell is a great fit for the rider and the horse. Saddle fitting is a delicate art and requires a lot of foresight and finesse. For their eBay customers, Trumbull Mountain can't physically check to make sure the saddle fits properly, and therefore they have published a helpful guide to proper saddle fitting on their eBay store. This page accomplishes two things. First, it helps saddle buyers know what to look for when buying a saddle. And second, it lets Trumbull Mountain's eBay shoppers know that the people at Trumbull Mountain are serious, helpful, and knowledgeable about saddle fitting. This separates them from the other bulk saddle sellers on eBay who are strictly interested in shipping as many out as possible.

If you sell clothing, consider posting a sizing and measurement chart for your customers. If you sell computer networking equipment, consider posting an overall network map detailing where each component fits in a system. The information on these pages may seem like common sense to you, but it could be extremely helpful to your buyers who don't deal with your products every day.

cHeckout

One of the most confusing aspects of shopping on eBay is that more often than not there are many checkout systems available for each seller. eBay provides its own electronic checkout system, third-party management services offer their own electronic checkout systems, and sellers often offer their own electronic checkout system on their web sites. Then buyers are also offered the options of paying by check, money order, credit card by telephone, wire transfer, and many others.

It is conceivable that one buyer of one item will have up to 10 available payment options. And these options will be different from seller to seller. This maze of payment options can begin to scare buyers away.

In addition to stating your payment policies on your listing pages, you should take the extra step of clearly stating your payment options with links to each checkout system. Include instructions for each checkout method so that no matter how a customer elects to pay you, they will have a clear idea of the process from start to finish.

It is great to make many methods of payment available to your customers, but there is something to be said for simplicity as well. I suggest sellers offer, at most, only three primary methods of payment: through PayPal, though your own checkout system, and by check.

You should offer PayPal simply because it is the standard on eBay and most buyers go shopping on eBay only because they have money to burn in their PayPal account. Buyers on eBay will expect you to accept it, and therefore you should. If you would like to provide a non-PayPal checkout system for your customers, I suggest you set up your own e-commerce checkout system on your business's web site. Using third-party checkout systems on unfamiliar web sites will scare away customers who are justifiably scared of online fraud. Finally, accepting checks will make your products available to folks who don't carry credit cards or flatly reject the idea of submitting financial information online. Their number are dwindling. But they exist.

cOnstant cOmmunication

It is extremely important to keep the lines of communication open during the course of a transaction. Unlike in your retail store where the transaction can take only a few seconds, selling an item on eBay can take up to 10 days. During this time you, or someone in your business, will need to be available to answer questions about your products, and the eBay process.

eBay provides their own message center through which buyers can semi-anonymously ask you questions about your products. You will receive an e-mail at your registered eBay e-mail address alerting you to the new message. Most often you will need to use eBay's message center to reply to these buyers. The process of logging back on to eBay and into the message center to answer questions can be much slower than simply replying through your e-mail program, but unfortunately, it is sometimes necessary.

There are methods you can use to speed up the question and answer process. By making more means of communication open to your customers, you can put yourself in a better position to answer questions quickly. First, you should post your business telephone number (along with your operating hours and time zone) on your listings. This will provide shoppers with an immediate and familiar way to contact you with questions.

You should post an eBay-specific e-mail address on all your listings and around your eBay pages as well. This could be "ebay@yourbusiness.com" or "tom@yourbusiness.com" or anything else as long as it is consistent across your eBay pages and is a frequently monitored address. By posting an e-mail address you are able to answer questions directly without needing to deal with eBay's often laborious message center.

One of the most exciting methods of communicating with customers was made possible when eBay purchased the Internet communications company Skype in October of 2005. Skype is a free VoIP (voice-over-Internet-protocol) program that has gained global popularity. Skype allows users with high-speed Internet access to speak to any other Skype user in the world—just as if over a telephone—for free. Skype also offers paid services that allow Skype users to call traditional telephones and vice versa.

The real benefit to eBay sellers is Skype's ability to enable instant, global, and free communication between buyers and sellers. Since buying Skype, eBay has been working on integrating it into its various marketplaces. By downloading Skype (at **www.skype.com**) and registering for a free account, you will be able to easily integrate this global communicator into your listings pages with eBay's help.

Once you've designated your Skype account name in your eBay settings, a Skype button will be placed on each of your item listing pages. Other Skype users around the world will be able to simply click this button on your pages and initiate a call to your computer. By clicking "answer" on your computer you will be able to speak directly with the caller through your computer's microphone and speakers. When the caller's question is answered, and the conversation is over, simply click "end call" to hang up. The caller could be in New Jersey or New Delhi, and the call is still free.

Now, speaking to customers through your computer's speakers and microphone might strike you as a low-quality approach to phone conversations—and you'd be right. Unless you've got incredible audio components on your desk at work, the sound quality would be poor on both ends of the conversation. Luckily, the rise in Skype's popularity is creating an entire industry of Skype-compatible audio components such as headsets, USB handsets, and more. Networking companies such as Netgear, Linksys, and D-Link are producing wireless technologies to help you carry a Skype phone around the office just as you would your regular cordless phone. Skype has an entire catalog of such gadgetry on their web site. If you think Skype is a great tool to integrate into your eBay sales, I suggest you upgrade your audio components to make sure that your call quality is up to professional standards.

Trumbull Mountain does not use Skype, as their only option for Internet connectivity is dial-up. Blue Star Computers uses Skype and finds it to be a great way to quickly answer questions for buyers, though they find that more often than not, buyers use Skype's text messaging capability before they use the program's voice calling function—which suits Blue Star just fine.

pOst-sAle cOmmunication

Post-sale communication is one area where many sellers fall behind. Many sellers fall into the trap of thinking that pre-sales communication is the most important and once the sale is successful, the communication can trail off. This is simply not the case. Communication must be strong at every stage of the transaction, especially at all points before the item is in the customer's hands.

Once a sale is made, your buyer should receive a "Congratulations" or "Thank You" e-mail with instructions on how to submit payment to you. This can be sent manually, or it can be automated by eBay's Selling Manager Pro or your eBay management service. If you choose to automate this e-mail, which I suggest you do, you should first edit it to ensure a friendly, nonautomated, tone.

After payment has been submitted to you, the buyer should receive a "Thank You for Your Payment" e-mail. In this e-mail your buyer should be notified of the item's expected ship date. This e-mail can be automated as well.

Once you have shipped the item, your buyer should be notified of the item's actual ship date, the selected carrier, the chosen service, the expected arrival time, and the item's tracking number. Providing a tracking number to your buyers for each shipment is a simple way to go above and beyond the normal service found on eBay. Buyers love watching their packages travel across the country to them, and it helps them to feel secure in their purchase.

After the package arrives at the buyer, it is at this point that you will most often receive feedback and complete the transaction. However, in some cases you will not hear from the buyer at all. This can mean two things. First, the buyer may be displeased with your product or customer service and chooses to bite his tongue instead of dinging you with negative feedback. Or second, the buyer simply forgot to leave you positive feedback after the sale. If you have not received feedback from a buyer after a few weeks of the item's delivery, you should send a carefully worded follow-up e-mail. You don't want to instigate a fight with unsatisfied buyers, and you don't want to annoy satisfied customers who have been busy with other things.

Trumbull Mountain found after a few months of selling that quite a large number of their buyers were not leaving them feedback at all. This can be quite annoying for sellers who work hard to impress customers to boost their feedback ratings, but then hear nothing back in return. Trumbull Mountain decided to send simple and brief follow-up e-mails to try to encourage satisfied customers to leave positive feedback and unsatisfied customers to contact them so that they could set things right. After getting into the habit of sending these e-mails, Trumbull Mountain's positive feedback rating began to climb higher, faster. Customers not only needed a reminder sometimes, but also appreciate that Trumbull Mountain followed up on their sales to make sure that everything was satisfactory.

---

tRumbull mOuntain's fOllow-up e-Mail

To: Buyer

From: Trumbull Mountain Tack Shop

Subject: Trumbull Mountain Tack Shop would love to hear from you!

Hello [Buyer's First Name],

Thanks again for your order from Trumbull Mountain Tack Shop. We appreciate your business and hope that your order arrived safely.

If you are happy with your order, we'd appreciate it if you could leave us some feedback on eBay. Each customer that provides us with positive feedback boosts our rating on eBay, and makes it possible for us to continue to serve the eBay community's equestrian needs.

If you are unhappy with your order or experience for any reason, please send us an e-mail so that we can make things right for you and improve our service.

Thanks again for your order.

Best,

Trumbull Mountain Tack Shop

---

rEturns

No seller wants to deal with returned items. A returned item means something went wrong along the way—a broken item, an incorrect shipment, an unsatisfied buyer. The key to running a successful returns operation is to set clear boundaries in your returns policy and state them clearly for your customers at every opportunity.

In the case of auction items, many of your items will likely be sold "as is." Many sellers will flat-out not accept returns on these items, to make sure that the item remains sold. This is a great way to both clean out a storeroom and scare off buyers. People, naturally, do not want to get stuck with an item they don't want, and will therefore avoid all 100% binding transactions. To open up "as is" auctions to more buyers, a new "as is" returns policy has evolved on eBay where returns are

On auction items that you'd really like to see go away and stay away, you can create a more customer-friendly returns policy than "you're stuck with it now buster!" For example, the following returns policy has evolved to suit the needs of eBay's unique selling environment.

"No returns accepted unless item is not as described."

not accepted on an item except where the item has not been accurately described. You'll see this returns policy more and more frequently on eBay now because it protects the seller from frivolous returns while at the same time providing recourse to a baffled buyer.

For your store items, you should have a more flexible returns policy. You will likely want your eBay's return policy to mirror your store's return policy. This will save you trouble when an eBay customer calls your store and inquires about your return policy. The inquiring customer could very easily get two different answers depending on who answers the phone—the eBay manager or your retail clerk. If you have one return policy that stretches across all sales channels, you won't run into this problem.

Clear communication should not be limited to interactions between your business and your customers. Internal communication must be efficient and clear as well. When adding eBay to your business, it is natural that some of your staff will know a lot about how eBay works while others will have no clue. Whether you try to avoid it or not, each of your staff members will, at some point, end up talking with one of your new eBay customers. Therefore it is vitally important that your staff be aware of your eBay operation's policies, processes, and products. If an uninformed staff member tells an inquiring eBay customer over the telephone that returns are accepted on all items—as is the case in your store—they may, in fact, be incorrectly informing the customer who purchased an "as is" closeout item at auction. Internal miscommunication will cause problems for your business.

Any eBay expansion needs to be a company-wide process. It isn't enough to have one eBay manager who knows about everything concerning eBay. You will be promoting your whole business on eBay. You universal contact information will be on display. Your whole company should be informed about your eBay operation.

cOnflict rEsolution

It is sad but true that you will inevitably run into problems and problem customers when doing business on eBay. Just like any other marketplace, eBay has its share of angry, pre-offended, unpleasant people who, it seems, exist to ruin your day. You have, no doubt, run into many of such people in your retail business and have your own methods for dealing with them. I defer to your best judgment in these situations, as I cannot offer any sage advice on dealing with unsavory characters that you don't already know.

However, I can clue you into how best to make use of eBay's tools to deal with these folks. The first things you should know is that feedback can only be left for you after a transaction has been made. If you find yourself confronted by a potential buyer before a sale is made, and you are convinced that the potential buyer will cause problems for you after the sale, it is possible to block specific users from being able to buy from you. In this way you can save yourself the trouble of selling to someone who may just be buying from you for the opportunity to leave negative feedback. Obviously, it is best to avoid pre-sales arguments as much as possible, but should one break out, you can protect yourself from spiteful feedback.

eBay does not often get involved in buyer-seller spats, though one situation in which they will is in the case of retaliatory feedback. If you, for any reason, leave negative feedback for a buyer, and then the buyer retaliates with negative feedback out of spite, eBay will remove their feedback at your request. In order for eBay to take action though, you must be able to prove that you did everything correctly on your end of the transaction.

Other situations in which eBay will get involved in conflicts include:

- eBay receives a court order to remove feedback that is libelous or illegal in some way.
- Feedback contains vulgar or hateful language.
- Feedback reveals personal information such as address or phone number.

Most potential arguments can be diffused through polite apologies and good customer service. The vast majority of shoppers on eBay are good-natured and simply looking for a bargain. Problems most often occur when sellers mistake a buyer's healthy suspicion of fraud as an attack on their integrity. Never lose sight of the marketplace in which you're selling. Customers have every right to be suspicious of mislabeled items or seemingly mispriced items. They're shopping on the Internet, where fraud is rampant. Try not to remove yourself so far from the buyer's perspective that you are unable separate your business presence on eBay from the larger context of the Internet.

You take pride in your business and will no doubt feel slighted when a buyer threatens to report you for listing an item they believe to be a fraud. But you must keep in mind that buyers like this have been burned on the Internet before and are simply scared. They don't know you from a hole in the ground. Try to see situations like this as an opportunity to improve that buyer's confidence in shopping online. Politely reply with all the pertinent information you can find that will help him or her to understand that the item, and your business, is very real. You may very well earn that customer's loyalty for life.

eChapter thirteen

In Closing

many businesses have expanded to eBay and found success. I have spoken with many of them at length and toured many of their operations in person. The one thing they each have in common is their enthusiasm for eBay. Each business I've met has expressed to me their excitement about the opportunities that eBay opens up for their once-local businesses. eBay has created an accessible open marketplace that stretches into nearly every economy in the world. The possibilities it represents for small businesses, and for your business, are real.

Capitalizing on any new opportunity requires planning, attention to details, and a good amount of hard work. eBay is no different. I hope this book has mapped out the eBay landscape for you in a way that makes your expansion process less of a mystery. The strategies and tools brought together for this book have been devised and tested by business owners just like you. They have been put to good use to turn small antique shops into eBay PowerSellers, and large companies into e-commerce powerhouses. I'm confident that in their most basic application, they will help your business grow. If you take the time and care necessary to refine these strategies to better fit your business model, they will help your business thrive.

Trumbull Mountain Tack Shop began this process with very little knowledge about eBay. Edie had purchased some boxes through the site in 2002 but had let her account go unused since then. Some of the other employees used eBay from time to time, but only for small purchases, and never to sell anything. They were, as a whole, inexperienced with eBay but understood the power of selling online due to the success of their own web site. They decided to test the waters on eBay to see if it held any potential for their products but wanted to do so in a professional, competent manner. I was lucky enough to be invited to monitor their progress.

The work of their expansion began in earnest in September of 2006. They put together their eBay Store, designed an auction template, and began listing their under-performing goods for a dollar. Items sold quickly, but by no means profitably. And because they were able to speak knowledgeably about their items, and shipped reliably, their feedback rating grew quickly.

With the growth of their feedback rating, so did the confidence of their buyers. They were gradually able to list and sell more expensive and more profitable items. When they earned their blue feedback star, they saw a boost in sales. When they listed more items in their store, they saw another boost in sales. By the end of their first month, they had sold just over $3,000 worth of goods with an average sale price of $70. At the end of October 2006, Trumbull Mountain had sold $4,800 worth of goods with an average sale price of $139.

In November their average sale price grew to $165. They were selling less, for more money. The venture was taking a turn for the profitable.

All along, a goal of theirs was to reach 100 feedback points. They reasoned that once they reached 100, they would have reasonably established themselves as a credible seller. They were right. Upon reaching 100 points in December, Trumbull Mountain saw another boost in sales.

Their December sales beat anyone's expectations. They had been able to sell, through their auctions and their store, over $10,000 worth of goods—more than double what they had sold in previous months—with an average sale price of $200.

Each month traffic to their items and to their store has doubled. Customers instantly began reacting to the professional approach that Trumbull Mountain brought to their eBay expansion and that I suggest throughout this book. They maintain a 100% positive feedback rating and are repeatedly thanked by customers for their friendly, knowledgeable service and fast shipping.

Truly Trumbull Mountain has done themselves proud. They approached their expansion in an intelligent, well-thought-out manner. They did all the research they could think to do. And while there were hiccups along the way, there's no question that they've been able to create a successful model for aspiring eBay business expansions.

As any seller on eBay knows, the PowerSeller title is really the gold crown for which they all strive. Many buyers refuse to purchase goods from any sellers who aren't PowerSellers, and therefore the PowerSeller badge translates to substantially more than an ego boost for the adorned company. Tangible financial benefits exist for PowerSellers. It is the last mark of credibility that buyers want to see before laying down their money.

It is no easy feat to achieve PowerSeller. Many books, articles, and web sites have been written about how to do it. Trumbull Mountain believed that the fastest path to PowerSeller for them was to put the strategies and tactics from this book to work. It was a difficult learning curve for many involved, but their work paid off. In early January, Trumbull Mountain received their invitation to the PowerSeller program from eBay—just four months after they began selling on eBay.

Along with the badge beside their username, Trumbull Mountain saw early January sales jump significantly. Instead of selling $2,000 or $3,000 per month as they were doing only a few months previously, Trumbull Mountain started the new year with two $5,000 weeks on eBay. Their new PowerSeller badge, and all their hard work that led up to it, was paying off.

Despite what the late-night and e-mail advertisers will tell you, there is no one secret to being successful on eBay. It is a combination of professionalism, hard work, and knowledge of the sales platform.

This book can provide you with proven strategies and a map of what's involved in selling on eBay, but the rest is up to you.

I wish you the best of luck in your expansion to eBay. It has proven successful for Blue Star Computer Corporation, West Barnstable Trading Company, Trumbull Mountain Tack Shop, and countless others. But please remember that for every business that succeeds on eBay, many others fail. It will be your dedication to making the expansion work and your enthusiasm for learning a new marketplace that will determine your outcome.

If you've found this book to be helpful, I'd like to hear from you. Please send any stories, tips, corrections, or other feedback to me at ebay@jsmcdougall.com. I wish you the best of luck in your expansion. I hope you find your success.

eBay Categories

the following is a list of eBay's main categories and first-level subcategories, with corresponding category numbers, as of December 2006. Categories come and go with market trends and the march of technology. Use this list as a reference when creating listings in third-party management software. Refer to **http://listings.ebay.com** for the most recent list.

Antiques (#20081)

Antiquities (Classical, Amer.) (#37903)

Architectural & Garden (#4707)

Asian Antiques (#20082)

Books, Manuscripts (#2195)

Decorative Arts (#20086)

Ethnographic (#2207)

Furniture (#20091)

Maps, Atlases, Globes (#37958)

Maritime (#37965)

Musical Instruments (#37974)

Primitives (#1217)

Rugs, Carpets (#37978)

Science & Medicine (#20094)

Silver (#20096)

Textiles, Linens (#2218)

Other Antiques (#12)

Art (#550)

Digital Art (#20118)

Drawings (#20119)

Folk Art (#357)

Mixed Media (#20122)

Paintings (#20125)

Photographic Images (#66465)

Posters (#28009)

Prints (#20140)

Sculpture, Carvings (#553)

Self-Representing Artists (#20158)

Other Art (#4174)

Wholesale Lots (#52524)

Baby (#2984)

Baby Gear (#100223)

Baby Safety & Health (#20433)

Bathing & Grooming (#20394)

Car Safety Seats (#66692)

Diapering (#45455)

Feeding (#20400)

Keepsakes & Baby Announcements (#117388)

Nursery Bedding (#20416)

Nursery Décor (#66697)

Nursery Furniture (#20422)

Potty Training (#37631)

Strollers (#66698)

Toys (#19068)

Other Baby Items (#1261)

Baby Wholesale Lots (#48757)

Books (#267)

Accessories (#45110)

Antiquarian & Collectible (#29223)
Audiobooks (#29792)
Catalogs (#118254)
Children's Books (#279)
Fiction Books (#377)
Magazine Back Issues (#280)
Magazine Subscriptions (#29253)
Nonfiction Books (#378)
Textbooks, Education (#2228)
Wholesale, Bulk Lots (#29399)
Other (#268)

Business & Industrial (#12576)
Agriculture & Forestry (#11748)
Construction (#11765)
Food Service & Retail (#11874)
Healthcare, Lab & Life Science (#11815)
Industrial Electrical & Test (#92074)
Industrial Supply, MRO (#1266)
Manufacturing & Metalworking (#11804)
Office, Printing & Shipping (#25298)
Other Industries (#26255)

Cameras & Photo (#625)
Bags, Cases & Straps (#107894)
Binoculars & Telescopes (#28179)
Camcorder Accessories (#11723)
Camcorders (#23781)
Digital Camera Accessories (#3327)
Digital Cameras (#29997)
Film (#4201)
Film Camera Accessories (#43478)
Film Cameras (#15230)
Film Processing & Darkroom (#15224)
Flashes & Accessories (#64353)
Lenses & Filters (#78997)

Lighting & Studio Equipment (#30078)

Manuals, Guides & Books (#4684)

Photo Albums & Archive Items (#29951)

Printers, Scanners & Supplies (#30021)

Professional Video Equipment (#21162)

Projection Equipment (#15250)

Stock Photography & Footage (#21198)

Tripods, Monopods (#30090)

Vintage (#3326)

Wholesale Lots (#45086)

Cell Phones & PDAs (#15032)

Accessories, Parts (#20336)

Bluetooth Wireless Accessories (#133225)

Cell Phones (#146487)

PDAs & Pocket PCs (#38331)

Phone & SIM Cards (#146492)

Wholesale & Large Lots (#45065)

Clothing, Shoes, & Accessories (#11450)

Infants & Toddlers (#3082)

Boys (#11452)

Girls (#11462)

Men's Accessories (#4250)

Men's Clothing (#1059)

Men's Shoes (#63850)

Uniforms (#28015)

Wedding Apparel (#3259)

Women's Accessories, Handbags (#4251)

Women's Clothing (#15724)

Women's Shoes (#63889)

Vintage (#110)

Wholesale, Large & Small Lots (#41964)

Coins & Paper Money (#11116)

Coins: US (#253)

Bullion (#39482)

Coins: Ancient (#4733)

Coins: World (#256)

Exonumia (#3452)

Paper Money: US (#3412)

Paper Money: World (#3411)

Publications & Supplies (#83274)

Scripophily (#3444)

Collectibles (#1)

Advertising (#34)

Animals (#1335)

Animation Art, Characters (#13658)

Arcade, Jukeboxes & Pinball (#66502)

Autographs (#14429)

Banks, Registers & Vending (#66503)

Barware (#3265)

Bottles & Insulators (#29797)

Breweriana, Beer (#562)

Casino (#898)

Clocks (#397)

Comics (#63)

Cultures, Ethnicities (#3913)

Decorative Collectibles (#13777)

Disneyana (#137)

Fantasy, Mythical & Magic (#10860)

Furniture, Appliances & Fans (#39629)

Historical Memorabilia (#13877)

Holiday, Seasonal (#907)

Housewares & Kitchenware (#13905)

Knives, Swords & Blades (#1401)

Lamps, Lighting (#1404)

Linens, Fabric & Textiles (#940)

Metalware (#1430)

Militaria (#13956)

Pens & Writing Instruments (#966)

Pez, Keychains, Promo Glasses (#14005)

Photographic Images (#14277)

Pinbacks, Nodders, Lunchboxes (#39507)

Postcards & Paper (#124)

Radio, Phonograph, TV, Phone (#29832)

Religions, Spirituality (#1446)

Rocks, Fossils, Minerals (#3213)

Science Fiction (#152)

Science, Medical (#412)

Tobacciana (#593)

Tools, Hardware & Locks (#13849)

Trading Cards (#868)

Transportation (#417)

Vanity, Perfume & Shaving (#597)

Vintage Sewing (#113)

Wholesale Lots (#45058)

Computers & Networking (#58058)

Apple, Macintosh Computers (#4599)

Desktop & Laptop Components (#3667)

Desktop & Laptop Accessories (#31530)

Desktop PCs (#3736)

Drives, Controllers & Storage (#165)

Laptops, Notebooks (#51148)

Monitors & Projectors (#3694)

Networking (#11176)

Printers (#1245)

Printer Supplies & Accessories (#11195)

Scanners (#11205)

Software (#18793)

Technology Books (#3516)

Vintage Computing Products (#11189)

Other Hardware & Services (#58059)

Consumer Electronics (#293)

> Car Electronics (#3270)
> DVD Players & Recorders (#32852)
> Digital Video Recorders, PVR (#32849)
> Gadgets & Other Electronics (#14948)
> GPS Devices (#34288)
> Home Audio (#14969)
> Home Theater in a Box (#39809)
> Home Theater Projectors (#48652)
> MP3 Players & Accessories (#97927)
> Portable Audio (#15052)
> Radios: CB, Ham & Shortwave (#1500)
> Satellite Radio (#60204)
> Satellite, Cable TV (#61383)
> Telephones & Pagers (#3286)
> Televisions (#11071)
> VCRs (#15088)
> Vintage Electronics (#14998)
> Wholesale Lots (#61494)

Crafts (#14339)

> Basketry (#134304)
> Bead Art (#31723)
> Candle & Soap Making (#28114)
> Ceramics, Pottery (#28121)
> Crocheting (#3094)
> Cross Stitch (#3091)
> Decorative, Tole Painting (#28126)
> Drawing (#28106)
> Embroidery (#28141)
> Fabric (#28155)
> Fabric Embellishments (#31727)
> Floral Crafts (#16491)
> Framing & Matting (#37573)
> General Art & Craft Supplies (#28102)
> Glass Art Crafts (#3100)

Handcrafted Items (#71183)

Kids Crafts (#116652)

Knitting (#3103)

Lacemaking, Tatting (#134590)

Latch Rug Hooking (#28147)

Leathercraft (#28131)

Macramé (#28151)

Metalworking (#41369)

Mosaic (#28134)

Needlepoint (#3104)

Paper Crafts (#134593)

Painting (#28110)

Quilting (#3111)

Ribbon (#83974)

Rubber Stamping & Embossing (#3122)

Scrapbooking (#11788)

Sewing (#3116)

Shellcraft (#3120)

Spinning (#36600)

Upholstery (#113354)

Weaving (#57739)

Woodworking (#3127)

Yarn (#36589)

Wall Décor, Tatouage (#75575)

Other Arts & Crafts (#75576)

Crafts Wholesale Lots (#45074)

Dolls & Bears (#237)

Bear Making Supplies (#50253)

Bears (#386)

Dolls (#238)

Dollhouse Miniatures (#1202)

Paper Dolls (#2440)

Wholesale Lots (#52546)

DVDs & Movies (#11232)

    DVD, HD DVD & Blu-ray (#617)

    Film (#63821)

    Laserdisc (#381)

    UMD (#132975)

    VHS (#309)

    VHS Non-US (PAL) (#1508)

    Other Formats (#41676)

    Wholesale Lots (#31606)

eBay Motors

    Motorcycles

    Parts & Accessories

    Passenger Vehicles

    Powersports

    Other Vehicles

Entertainment Memorabilia (#45100)

    Autographs-Original (#57)

    Autographs-Reprints (#104412)

    Movie Memorabilia (#196)

    Music Memorabilia (#2329)

    Television Memorabilia (#1424)

    Theater Memorabilia (#2362)

    Video Game Memorabilia (#45101)

    Other Memorabilia (#2312)

Gift Certificates (#31411)

Health & Beauty (#26395)

    Bath & Body (#11838)

    Coupons (#82567)

    Dietary Supplements, Nutrition (#19259)

    Fragrances (#26396)

    Hair Care (#11854)

    Hair Removal (#31762)

    Health Care (#67588)

Makeup (#31786)

Nail (#11871)

Massage (#36447)

Medical, Special Needs (#11778)

Natural Therapies (#67659)

Oral Care (#31769)

Over-the-Counter Medicine (#75036)

Skin Care (#11863)

Tanning Beds, Lamps (#31775)

Tattoos, Body Art (#33914)

Vision Care (#31414)

Weight Management (#31817)

Wholesale Lots (#40965)

Other Health & Beauty Items (#1277)

Home & Garden (#11700)

Bath (#20438)

Bedding (#20444)

Building & Hardware (#3187)

Dining & Bar (#71236)

Electrical & Solar (#20595)

Food & Wine (#14308)

Furniture (#3197)

Gardening & Plants (#2032)

Heating, Cooling & Air (#41986)

Home Decor (#10033)

Home Security (#41968)

Kitchen (#20625)

Lamps, Lighting, Ceiling Fans (#20697)

Major Appliances (#20710)

Outdoor Power Equipment (#29518)

Patio & Grilling (#20716)

Pet Supplies (#1281)

Plumbing & Fixtures (#20601)

Pools & Spas (#20727)

Rugs & Carpets (#20584)

Tools (#631)

Vacuum Cleaners & Housekeeping (#299)

Window Treatments (#63514)

Wholesale Lots (#31605)

Jewelry & Watches (#281)

Body Jewelry (#10968)

Bracelets (#10975)

Charms & Charm Bracelets (#3835)

Children's Jewelry (#84605)

Designer Brands (#11317)

Earrings (#10985)

Ethnic, Tribal Jewelry (#11312)

Hair Jewelry (#110620)

Handcrafted, Artisan Jewelry (#110633)

Jewelry Boxes & Supplies (#10321)

Loose Beads (#488)

Loose Diamonds & Gemstones (#491)

Men's Jewelry (#10290)

Necklaces & Pendants (#10994)

Pins, Brooches (#11008)

Rings (#67725)

Sets (#43209)

Vintage, Antique (#48579)

Watches (#14324)

Other Items (#505)

Wholesale Lots (#40131)

Music (#11233)

Accessories (#52473)

Cassettes (#1600)

CDs (#307)

Digital Music Downloads (#88451)

DVD Audio (#46353)

Records (#306)

Super Audio CDs (#46354)
Other Formats (#618)
Wholesale Lots (#31608)

Musical Instruments (#619)

Brass (#16212)
DJ Gear & Lighting (#14982)
Electronic (#38068)
Equipment (#41402)
Guitar (#3858)
Harmonica (#47078)
Instruction Books, CDs, Videos (#100228)
Keyboard, Piano (#16217)
Percussion (#10172)
Pro Audio (#15197)
Sheet Music, Song Books (#20833)
String (#10176)
Woodwind (#10181)
Wholesale Lots (#52555)
Other Instruments (#308)

Pottery & Glass (#870)

Glass (#50693)
Pottery & China (#18875)

Real Estate (#10542)

Commercial (#15825)
Land (#15841)
Manufactured Homes (#94825)
Residential (#12605)
Timeshares for Sale (#15897)
Other Real Estate (#1607)

Specialty Services (#316)

Advice & Instruction (#50337)
Artistic Services (#47126)
Custom Clothing & Jewelry (#50343)

eBay Auction Services (#50349)
Graphic & Logo Design (#47131)
Media Editing & Duplication (#50355)
Printing & Personalization (#20943)
Restoration & Repair (#47119)
Web & Computer Services (#47104)
Other Services (#317)

Sporting Goods (#382)

Athletic Apparel (#137006)
Athletic Footwear (#137010)
Airsoft (#31680)
Archery (#20835)
Baseball & Softball (#16021)
Basketball (#21194)
Billiards (#21209)
Bowling (#20846)
Boxing (#30100)
Camping, Hiking, Backpacking (#16034)
Canoes, Kayaks, Rafts (#36121)
Climbing (#30105)
Cycling (#7294)
Disc Golf (#79802)
Equestrian (#3153)
Exercise & Fitness (#15273)
Fishing (#14104)
Football (#21214)
Go-Karts, Recreational (#64655)
Golf (#1513)
Gymnastics (#79792)
Hunting (#7301)
Ice, Roller Hockey (#40154)
Ice Skating (#21225)
Indoor Games (#36274)
Inline, Roller Skating (#16258)
Lacrosse (#62163)

Martial Arts (#36279)

Paintball (#16045)

Racquetball & Squash (#62166)

Running (#64685)

Scooters (#11330)

Scuba, Snorkeling (#16052)

Skateboarding (#16262)

Skiing & Snowboarding (#36259)

Snowmobiling (#23831)

Soccer (#20862)

Surfing, Wind Surfing (#22709)

Swimming (#74050)

Tennis (#20868)

Triathlon (#64680)

Wakeboarding, Waterskiing (#23806)

Other Sports (#40141)

Wholesale Lots (#40146)

Sports Mem, Cards & Fan Shop (#64482)

Autographs-Original (#51)

Autographs-Reprints (#50115)

Cards (#212)

Fan Apparel & Souvenirs (#24409)

Game Used Memorabilia (#50116)

Manufacturer Authenticated (#60591)

Vintage Sports Memorabilia (#50123)

Wholesale Lots (#56080)

Stamps (#260)

United States (#261)

Australia (#3468)

Canada (#3478)

Br. Comm. Other (#263)

UK (Great Britain) (#3499)

Africa (#692)

Asia (#47174)

Europe (#4742)

Latin America (#4747)

Middle East (#3491)

Publications & Supplies (#704)

Topical & Specialty (#4752)

Worldwide (#352)

Tickets (#1305)

Event Tickets (#16122)

Experiences (#16071)

Other Items (#1306)

Toys & Hobbies (#220)

Action Figures (#246)

Beanbag Plush, Beanie Babies (#49019)

Building Toys (#18991)

Classic Toys (#19016)

Diecast, Toy Vehicles (#222)

Educational (#11731)

Electronic, Battery, Wind-Up (#19071)

Fast Food, Cereal Premiums (#19077)

Games (#233)

Model RR, Trains (#479)

Models, Kits (#1188)

Outdoor Toys, Structures (#11743)

Pretend Play, Preschool (#19169)

Puzzles (#2613)

Radio Control (#2562)

Robots, Monsters, Space Toys (#19192)

Slot Cars (#2616)

Stuffed Animals (#436)

Toy Soldiers (#2631)

Trading Card Games (#2536)

TV, Movie, Character Toys (#2624)

Vintage, Antique Toys (#717)

Wholesale Lots (#40149)

Travel (#3252)

Airline (#3253)

Car Rental (#147399)

Cruises (#16078)

Lodging (#16079)

Luggage (#16085)

Vacation Packages (#29578)

Other Travel (#1310)

Video Games (#1249)

Accessories (#49220)

Games (#62053)

Internet Games (#1654)

Systems (#62054)

Vintage Games (#4315)

Other (#187)

Wholesale Lots (#48749)

Everything Else (#99)

Advertising Opportunities (#102333)

eBay User Tools (#20924)

Education & Learning (#16706)

Funeral & Cemetery (#88739)

Genealogy (#20925)

Gifts & Occasions (#16086)

Information Products (#102480)

Mature Audiences (#319)

Memberships (#16709)

Metaphysical (#19266)

Mystery Auctions (#102534)

Personal Security (#102535)

Religious Products & Supplies (#102545)

Reward Pts, Incentive Progs (#102553)

Test Auctions (#14112)

Weird Stuff (#1466)

Other (#88433)

eAppendix b

Associated Fees

following is a listing of the fees associated with selling on eBay. These fees are subject to change and often do change. Please check **http://pages.ebay.com/help/sell/fees.html** for a list of eBay's most current fees.

Insertion Fees	
Starting or Reserve Price	**Insertion Fee**
$0.01–$0.99	$0.20
$1.00–$9.99	$0.35
$10.00–$24.99	$0.60
$25.00–$49.99	$1.20
$50.00–$199.99	$2.40
$200.00–$499.99	$3.60
$500.00 or more	$4.80

Final Value Fees	
Closing Price	**Final Value Fee**
Item not sold	No fee
$0.01–$25	5.25% of the closing value
$25.01–$1,000	5.25% of the initial $25 ($1.31), plus 3.00% of the remaining closing value balance ($25.01–$1,000)
Equal to or over $1000.01	5.25% of the initial $25 ($1.31), plus 3.00% of the initial $25.01–$1,000 ($29.25), plus 1.50% of the remaining closing value balance ($1000.01-closing value)

Business & Industrial Capital Equipment Category Specific Fees	
Insertion Fee	$20
Reserve Fees	$5
Final Value Fees	1.00% of the closing value (maximum charge $250.00)

Insertion and Transaction Service Fee, eBay Motors		
Category	**Insertion Fee**	**Transaction Services Fee**
Passenger Vehicles	$40	$40
Motorcycles	$30	$30
Powersports	$30	$30
Powersports Vehicles Under 50cc	$3	$3
Other Vehicles	$40	$40
Parts and Accessories	Same as eBay.com Insertion Fees	

Subscription Fees, All eBay Stores	
Store Level	**Fee**
Basic	$15.95/month
Featured	$49.95/month
Anchor	$499.95/month

Insertion Fees, All eBay Stores		
Starting or Reserve Price	**30 days**	**Good Until Cancelled***
$0.01–$24.99	$0.05	$0.05/30 days
$25.00–and above	$0.10	$0.15/30 days

*Good Until Cancelled listings will be charged the relevant fees every 30 days.

Final Value Fees, eBay Stores	
Closing Price	**Final Value Fee**
Item Not Sold	No Fee
$0.01–$25	10.00% of the closing price
$25.01–$100	10.00% of the initial $25 ($2.50), plus 7.00% of the remaining closing value balance
$100.01–$1,000	10.00% of the initial $25.00 ($2.50), plus 7.00% of the initial $25.01–$100 ($5.25), plus 5.00% of the remaining closing value balance $100.01–$1,000
Over $1,000.01	10.00% of the initial $25 ($2.50), plus 7.00% of the initial $25.01–$100 ($5.25), plus 5.00% of the initial $100.01–$1,000, plus 3.00% of the remaining closing value balance ($1,000.01–closing value)

Ad Format Fee	
Ad Format Listing Type	
Duration	**Insertion Fee**
30-day listing	$9.95
60-day listing	$19.90
90-day listing	$29.85

Real Estate Fees		
Timeshare, Land, and Manufactured Homes		
Listing Type	**Duration**	**Insertion Fee**
Auction Format	1-, 3-, 5-, 7-, or 10-day listing	$35
Auction Format	30-day listing	$50
Ad Format	30-day listing	$150
Ad Format	90-day listing	$300

Real Estate Fees		
Residential, Commercial, and Other Real Estate		
Listing Type	**Duration**	**Insertion Fee**
Auction Format	1-, 3-, 5-, 7-, or 10-day listing	$100
Auction Format	30-day listing	$150
Ad Format	30-day listing	$150
Ad Format	90-day listing	$300

Real Estate Fees	
Final Value Fee	
Item Category	**Notice Fee**
Timeshares, Land, and Manufactured Homes	$35
Residential, Commercial and Other	No Fee

PayPal Fees	
Transaction Fees for Domestic (US) Payments	
Monthly Sales	**Price Per Transaction**
$0.01–$3,000	2.9% + $0.30
$3,000.01–$10,000	2.5% + $0.30
$10,000.01–$100,000	2.2% + $0.30
$100,000.00 and above	1.9% + $0.30

eAppendix c

eBay Tools

to make the most of your time selling on eBay, you should take advantage of some of the various tools that are available to sellers. eBay and third-party software developers have created an industry of eBay-helper software. You can find tools to help you manage your listings, your client communication, your shipping, and much more. The following is a directory for you to use as a reference when looking for new tools to help you succeed on eBay. Each of the following entries is a tool that I've found useful or was recommended to me by one of the PowerSellers I've interviewed for this or other books. In the spirit of eBay's feedback star system, I've assigned each entry a star rating.

Star Rating Key

★ = Recommended with some reservations

★★ = Recommended

★★★ = Highly recommended

★★★★ = Go now, get it

accounting

KeepMore.net: This service has recognized and addressed the lack of worthwhile eBay-specific accounting programs available. If you have decided to make your eBay operation independent of your main accounting system, this service holds some promise. KeepMore.net allow for easy importing of your eBay sales and generates numerous helpful profitability reports for you to study. KeepMore.net also makes tax time easier by filling out tax forms for you.
Rating: ★

Zoovy.com: Zoovy is an eBay-certified solutions provider as well as an Intuit-certified solution provider. They provide an eBay accounting service with QuickBooks integration, which can make life easier for you if you are already using QuickBooks to track your business's expenses.
Rating: ★

activity monitoring

AuctionMonitor.net: This service offers a variety of tools to help buyers and sellers watch their auctions. They offer widgets for Mac OS X Tiger and Yahoo! Widgets to allow you access to your auctions right from your desktop. They also provide RSS feeds of your auction information, allowing you to add your auction information to any of the RSS reading services around the Internet, such as your Google Homepage, or your My Yahoo! page. Their new web site display service allows you to place your auction information on your own web site. This could be very helpful for sellers.
Rating: ★★

BayToGo.com: This service will alert you via a text message to your mobile phone, pager, or PDA when your auctions receive bids or ends. You can also configure BayToGo to send alerts to an e-mail address. You are able to specify a daily time-frame within which to receive notifications so that your phone isn't beeping all night long.
Rating: ★★

AuctionMessenger.net: This service provides a download application for Windows PCs that resembles an instant messenger program. However, instead of "buddies" in your Buddy List, Auction Messenger displays up-to-date auction information.
Rating: ★★

communication

Skype.com: Skype is eBay's voice-over-Internet-protocol (VOIP) program. This free download allows buyers with Skype to make free voice calls to sellers who have integrated the program into their auctions and contact information—a process that eBay has made simple. Skype makes free voice, instant message, and video communication with buyers around the globe possible.
Rating: ★★★★

Selling Manager Pro: eBay's Selling Manager Pro has streamlined client communication by tracking and managing customer correspondence. Selling Manager Pro will alert you when a customer has a question, keep track of which questions you have answered, and suggest when you should contact various buyers with certain types of information—such as tracking numbers and receipts. Selling Manager Pro will also automate and customize many e-mails during the post-sale process.
Rating: ★★★

Andale's Customer Manager: Andale (pronounced: ON-duh-lay) provides a full-scale customer relationship manager. This service manager enables you to collect information from your buyers, organize buyers into mailing lists, and even sends birthday reminders when it is time. You can automate many of Andale's customer management services to occur when you need them to, without the need for input from you.
Rating: ★★

finding products

Liquidation.com: Many large businesses turn to Liquidation.com to help them clean out their inventories of dead stock, their offices of unused computers, and their warehouses of returned goods. The quality of product you will find here will vary. However, the site uses a seller rating system similar to eBay's so that you can investigate a seller's history before laying down thousands of dollars for 10 pallets of broken DVD players.

Rating: ★

worldwidebrands.com: Worldwide Brands, Inc. was started by eBay guru Chris Malta. He has built a large database of reliable wholesalers with the specific intention of providing eBay sellers with products to sell. This service is highly recommended by eBay, Inc. Sellers can search for products from drop-shippers, light bulk wholesalers, and more. Memberships are sold as one-time payments that give you access for life.

Rating: ★★★★

andale.com: Andale also offers their Andale Suppliers service. This is a simple service wherein you create a profile specifying what you would like to sell on eBay, and suppliers of that item are encouraged to contact you. You may also search within Andale's supplier network for suppliers of your desired items.

Rating: ★★★

Honesty.com: Popping up across the Internet now are eBay "Deal Finders." Basically, eBay research companies have figured out a way to sell information to both sellers and buyers. They present information about the most profitable items to sellers, and now, opposite information about the least profitable to buyers. Honesty.com, and its sister site Dealio.com—both operated by Andale, can be a good places to hunt for items to buy low and resell high.

Rating: ★★

photo hosting

villagephotos.net: This service allows eBay sellers without their own web sites to present as many photos as they would like on their auctions without paying more per photo. Villagephotos.net uses a simple interface for photo management. Users can upload their photos through their web browser or with an FTP client for faster transfers. Simple image editing tools such as resizing, compression, and thumbnail creation are also available.

Rating: ★

albumpost.com: This service is not specifically intended to help eBay sellers host their item images, but it does just that perfectly well. Albumpost offers unlimited storage, which your own web host most likely will not provide. This means that you can host all of your item images in one place without the need to pay for extra storage or transfer capacity. Albumpost's FAQ page walks eBay sellers through the process of integrating their albumpost photos into their eBay auctions.

Rating: ★★★

software integration

eBay's Accounting Assistant: This tool is provided by eBay at no cost to subscribers of eBay's Stores program, Selling Manager Pro, Seller's Assistant Basic, and Seller's Assistant Pro. It is a simple program that is integrated with eBay and exports your sales data into a format that QuickBooks can read.

Rating: ★★

listing management

eBay's TurboLister: TurboLister is a download application for Windows PCs. It is the most widely used and most trusted listing management program. You'll find that because it is published by eBay, it enjoys some advantages that third-party listing management serv-

ices don't, such as faster and frequent updates, near seamless integration, and support from eBay's support team. It is a free download, and available at **http://pages.ebay.com/turbo_lister**.
Rating: ★★

eBay's Blackthorne Pro: This is another download application published by the eBay software development team. This is an all-in-one selling solution that has capabilities that extend beyond TurboLister's basic listing tools. Blackthorne Pro offers listing creation, inventory management, monthly profit and loss reports, and supplier management. This is the management program in use by Blue Star Computers. They find it to be well-done overall, but buggy in places and a gigantic memory hog. If you plan on running Blackthorne Pro, upgrade your computer first. Learn more at **http://pages.ebay.com/blackthorne/pro.html**.
Rating: ★

Auctiva: Auctiva is a completely free listing management service. They provide the basic tool set: WYSIWYG HTML creation, a template library, cross-references, and listing management. Every listing you create through Auctiva will have their logo and promotions inserted at the bottom. This can be a deterrent for sellers who spent big money customizing and perfecting their templates. However, for the lower-budget sellers, a free listing management solution can be quite handy.
Rating: ★

ChannelAdvisor Pro: Trumbull Mountain began their eBay expansion process using ChannelAdvisor Pro. They found the service's listing creating and management tools to be the best of the web-based services available. The photo and template managers are incredibly easy to learn and use, and the auction traffic statistics are well displayed. They offer no accounting reports and their inventory manager can be frustrating, but in terms of listing management, they excel. Visit them at **www.channeladvisor.com**.
Rating: ★★

Andale: Andale's Lister service is a web-based eBay management platform. Included in your Lister subscription is the ability to use Lister

Pro, Andale's download application for Windows PCs. The data you enter into either platform (web-based or desktop application) does not sync between the two. So for the one price you can use one or the other. Andale has included many features and resources that eBay's Selling Manager Pro and TurboLister do not offer. The competing services are similarly priced, but Andale comes out on top feature-wise. Andale also offers far more subscription levels than eBay, so that you will have an easier time selecting one that most closely meets your needs.
Rating: ★★★

eBay's File Exchange: The File Exchange service is aimed at sellers who would prefer to use their favorite non-eBay specific program to manage their eBay inventory. This program could be a spreadsheet application, a database manager, or even just a text editor. File Exchange is compatible with nearly any application on any operating system. This is a web-based tool that you would use to create a listing document template. You base your listing file off this template and then upload the whole file to eBay. File Exchanger reads the data in the file and creates listings from the entries you've created. Some seller restrictions apply. Visit **http://pages.ebay.com/file_exchange** for more information.
Rating: ★

research

Andale: Andale's Research Tool is the most helpful I've tested. For the low price of $7.95 per month, this service will give you access to important information regarding an unlimited number of items. Andale's Research Tool is in its second version and will provide you with numbers and graphs detailing the following information: average selling price, number of items listed, number of items sold, success rate of item, the best time to sell, the best format to use, the best upgrades to select, the best starting price, and more. For an extra fee, you can subscribe to Andale's What's Hot service, which will alert you to growing trends on eBay so that you can fully capitalize when it arrives.
Rating: ★★★★

Marketplace Research: eBay's Marketplace Research tool is helpful for your basic research needs. If you are only seeking quick information to make preliminary decisions about whether or not to sell an item, then Marketplace Research will help you. If you need more than cursory information, this service will leave you wanting for more. eBay offers several subscription plans, including two-day plans for fast research.
Rating: ★

HammerTap: Despite its silly name, HammerTap offers a serious service. They offer one of the oldest and most trusted eBay research services available. eBay aficionados recommend it often. Their Deep Analysis program will show you what's selling, when it's selling, and how to sell it. It takes all the guesswork out of profiting. HammerTap is a download application for Windows PCs. Find out more at **www.hammertap.com**.
Rating: ★★★★

Terapeak.com: Terapeak offers an eBay research suite as well. They offer much of the same analysis as eBay's Marketplace Research, with similar pricing. Terapeak offers a free 10-day trial period, which is exactly the amount of time I used their service. I was not disappointed, but I was not impressed either. Decide for yourself at **www.terapeak.com**.
Rating: ★★

Shipping

Shipping Center: eBay provides a Shipping Center suite of tools to help make your shipping operation easier. They offer shipping calculators, package tracking, label printing, and links to eBay's UPS Shipping Zone and USPS Shipping Zone—both utilities to help sellers integrate these companies into their operations. Many of these services should be included in your eBay management software, if you choose to use some. If not, this shipping center can be helpful. Learn more at **http://pages.ebay.com/services/buyandsell/shipping.html**.
Rating: ★★

redroller.com: Red Roller provides a complete selling management solution for free to eBay sellers. They boast that they are able to save sellers an average of 30% on shipping costs through their comparison shipping shopping utility. Their services include: rate comparisons, address book, eBay integration, e-mail notifications, and a package tracking manager. Learn more at **www.redroller.com**.
Rating: ★★★

ClearPath: Pitney Bowes has created their ClearPath service to help sellers ship internationally—a process that usually involves considerable risk, cumbersome paperwork, and expensive customs fees. The burden of preparing packages to ship overseas is so great on small businesses that many sellers elect to limit their shipping to domestic sales—ignoring the huge international market. ClearPath provides the solution. This service will tackle the most laborious parts of the process for you. ClearPath calculates your total passage fees, fills out all the necessary paperwork, and even saves you money on border taxes. You ship to ClearPath's domestic location, and they send it overseas to your customer. This is a wonderful service and I highly recommend it for the huge markets it makes accessible and for the overall ease of use of the service. Learn more at **www.pbclearpath.com/sellerzone**.
Rating: ★★★★

eAppendix d

Common eBay Abbreviations

eBay has grown so large that it has begun to develop its own culture and language. Communication constraints within the eBay community have led to the mutation of conventional English. The following acronyms are used across eBay where character limits, or time constraints, restrict language—most often in auction titles. The following list of acronyms are generally safe to use. For the current version of eBay-approved acronyms, visit **http://pages.ebay.com/help/newtoebay/acronyms.html**.

B&W: Black and white
BC: Back cover
BIN: Buy It Now
CIP: Customer initiated payment
DOA: Dead on arrival
EST: Eastern Standard Time
EUC: Excellent used condition
FAQ: A list of frequently asked questions with answers
FB: Feedback
FC: Fine condition
FVF: Final Value Fee

G: Good condition

GBP: Great Britain Pounds

GU: Gently Used. Item that has been used but shows little wear, accompanied by explanation of wear.

HP: Home page

HTF: Hard to find

HTML: Hypertext Markup Language. The language used to create web pages.

IE: Internet Explorer

INIT: Initials

ISP: Internet Service Provider: a company that gives you access to the Internet

JPG: Preferred file format for pictures on eBay (pronounced "Jay-Peg")

LTBX: Letterbox. Video format that recreates a widescreen image

LTD: Limited edition

MNT: Mint. In perfect condition (a subjective term)

MIB: Mint in box

MIJ: Made in Japan

MIMB: Mint in mint box

MIMP: Mint in mint package

MIP: Mint in package

MNB: Mint no box

MOC: Mint on card

MOMC: Mint on mint card

MONMC: Mint on near-mint card

MWBT: Mint with both tags

MWMT: Mint with mint tags

NARU: Not a registered user (or suspended user)

NBW: Never been worn

NC: No cover

NIB: New in box

NM: Near mint

NOS: New old stock

NR: No reserve price for an auction-style listing

NRFB: Never removed from box

NWT: New with tags

NWOT: New without original tags

OEM: Original equipment manufacturer

OOP: Out of print

PL: A Pink or a Pinkliner. This refers to an eBay staff member who posts a message on a Discussion Board. Messages from eBay staff have a pink header.

PM: Priority Mail

PST: Pacific Standard Time

RET: Retired

SCR: Scratch

S/O: Sold out

Sig: Signature

SYI: Sell Your Item form

TM: Trademark

UPI: Unpaid Item

URL: Uniform Resource Locator. The address that identifies a web site (such as **www.ebay.com**).

USPS: United States Postal Service

VF: Very fine condition

VHTF: Very hard to find

WS: Widescreen (same as letterbox)

XL: Extra large

Index